THE
Supra-Natural
LIFE

Where Word and Spirit Meet

Christen Forster

INTEGRITY
MEDIA EUROPE

Integrity Media Europe
Unit 1 Hargreaves Business Park
Hargreaves Road
Eastbourne
BN23 6QW

www.integrityeurope.com
www.iworship24-7.com

All Scripture quotations are based on the author's own translation.

ISBN 978-1-907080-29-6

Printed and bound in the UK by CPI Antony Rowe,
Chippenham and Eastbourne
Cover design by CCD, www.ccdgroup.co.uk

Contents

What Others Are Saying
About *The Supra-Natural Life*

"Christen brings a multi-faceted revelation concerning how to naturally live an unprecedented Christian life by the power of the Holy Spirit. I highly recommend this outstanding book."
Ché Ahn, *Senior Pastor, HROCK Church, Pasadena, CA. President, Harvest International Ministry. International Chancellor, Wagner Leadership Institute*

"Christen's insights and understanding of spiritual transformation and growth are profound. In this easy-to-read book he brings Scripture alive and imparts fresh revelation to help us live a 'Supra-natural life'."
Stephen Klemich, *Founder of Achievement Concepts and HeartStyles*
Dr. Mara Klemich PhD, *Psychologist and co-founder of HeartStyles*

"Christen has painted a picture of the supra-natural life with a wonderful balance of stirring challenge and encouraging accessibility. I thoroughly recommend both reading and living this message."
Richard Pennystan, *Associate Vicar - ChristChurch Fulham*

"A thought-provoking book which is both dynamic and powerful, combining personal stories with insightful truths. I recommend that everyone read it and allow the seeds of reality to grow within you."
Tim Eldridge, *Senior Leader of Harrogate New Life Church and Founder of Kingdom Connections*

"This wonderful book is the product of a life rich in testimony, wisdom revelation and inheritance. It cannot fail to invite you to a greater awareness of living a life above the natural. But I believe it will do more than that, because the author has lived this journey. There is an impartation to be given well beyond the mere reading of the book. I invite you to read it, but as you do, receive from it and the author the *supra-natural anointing* to live this life for yourself."
Paul Manwaring, *Bethel Church, Redding, CA.*

Dedication

For my fantastic wife, Judith,
who has taught me more than anyone else
how to live life in Technicolor!

Acknowledgments and Thanks

It is good to be grateful. It connects us to other people and to our Maker. In writing this book, I have been reminded of just how much I owe to so many for the life that I have - the life that has given me the experiences, ability and space to write.

First, there are those who have most directly helped in producing this book. Foremost of these is Ann Handford, who not only organised my life so that I had the time to write, but also pushed the project along, booking me time away and keeping me accountable to a schedule. Then there are friends who reviewed and critiqued material: Fran Stedman, Dave Smith and Ben Trigg. So a big thank you to you all!

Then there is my family. First, thanks to my parents, Roger and Faith, who lived an inspirational life and gave me more than just foundations for my own faith. They will no doubt spot their influence in this book. In the opposite direction I want to thank my three children, Joel, Kezia and Olivia, who have given me the opportunity to see life from Father's perspective. Then my wonderful wife, Judith, who has had to pay the biggest price to help me become who I am today. Judith, I learnt most of my heart lessons with you and from you!

Finally, I want to thank all those who have been part of my church community in River and Ichthus. I have either learnt from you or tried out on you so much of what is in this book.

And then there is Jesus!

Foreword

As I read this book, I experienced, again and again, a deep "YES!" in my mind and spirit.

I have known Christen Forster for a long time. I first met his father, Roger, in 1972 shortly after my wife and I moved to London to pioneer the work of Youth With A Mission in England. Some years later, Christen came to my attention when I learned that Roger's teenage son had been diagnosed with cancer. Two of my friends believed that God had spoken to them to go and pray for Christen, so they obeyed and Christen was healed. At the time, I wondered what God had in mind for this young man. I knew he had wonderful parents and a great Christian heritage.

About ten years later, I began to work with Christen in the church-planting movement Challenge 2000 and came to appreciate his wide-ranging abilities and leadership gifts. We were doing things together and it was satisfying to see all the results. But one of our weaknesses in the evangelical churches in western nations is that DOING can eclipse our call to BE like Jesus. In that sense, Christen and I walked a similar road for another decade or so.

But, God is gracious and patient with us. His overarching purpose of making us like Jesus cannot be permanently obscured. He has many ways of confronting us with His central purpose of continually changing us to become more like Christ. One of those ways is failure. I suppose casual observers of my life and ministry in Youth With A Mission would not have described it as failure. But I was frustratingly aware of having to work harder and harder for less results. In our activist, missionary lives, success is measured by observable fruit – people being converted, new missionaries being recruited and trained, new ministries being pioneered and numerical growth. But the numbers weren't great and the load was heavy.

Then one of my projects took me to the Middle East for long periods of time and I began to get to know Christians who had lived as a struggling minority for generations. They are not usually activists, but their focus was often on being transformed into the image of Christ. Their lives stood as a rebuke to mine (although they sometimes felt that my activism was an example to them!) Through fellowship, reading their books, using their prayers and sitting at the feet of able teachers, I began to walk the path that Christen walked and reveals in this book.

It is true that the "abundant life" we pursue as believers in Jesus is not always what we expect. Often, as Christen and I experienced for a time, we can miss out on what He has for us because we have our own preconceptions of what it should look like. Letting go of our own ideas about how we can see more of the Spirit of God at work in our lives and learning to let the Holy Spirit make it actually happen is a process. Christen openly and humbly demonstrates that this is a journey that can be wrought with challenges, but also one that any of us are invited to take. In his genuine, identifiable experiences, any of us can recognise the longing for a life that is more like the one Jesus described.

Most believers will have read the passages about being "transformed from one degree of glory to the next", about Jesus and the Father "making their home in us", and about together, being a "living temple" for the presence of God. But somehow, that knowledge has to move from a general awareness to a deep conviction that provides a life-long focus. When it does, then the days of boring Christian life are over! There is no greater adventure than this.

Lynn Green
International Director, YWAM

Series
Introduction

In March 1965, Goldie, a Golden Eagle escaped from London Zoo. Though it happened a year before I was born, I remember as a child watching the retelling of the story of his escape on the children's magazine show "Blue Peter". For twelve days Goldie hung around in the trees of London's Regents Park, where hunger drove him to attack a couple of Yorkshire Terriers and eat a duck who lived in the garden of the American Ambassador's house. Goldie was recaptured when he spied a dead rabbit that had been tethered to the ground by his keeper.

During his bid for freedom, there were several traffic-jams around the park as crowds of people flocked to see this magnificent bird flying free. But watching the TV footage you can't help feeling that they must have been a bit disappointed. Goldie didn't behave like a Golden Eagle soaring majestically in open skies, roosting on mountain-tops and cliff edges. He lived his twelve days of freedom like a big pigeon hopping from tree-top to tree-top, never venturing far from home and only occasionally flirting with what he could be. That said, Goldie obviously enjoyed his freedom because in December of the same year he escaped again. This time the sweet breeze of liberty gusted under his wings for a mere four days before his re-capture.

Over my years of following Jesus, I have often applied the meta-phor of Goldie the Golden Eagle and his great escape to my own life and to the lives of others. We know we are free and we love our freedom. We look up at the sky above us and feel the "upward call of God" (Philippians 3:14), but we are not sure what we are sup-posed to do with the freedom Jesus has won for us.

It is much easier to know what we have been set free from, than it is to know what we have been set free for!

Jesus said He had come to give us an abundant life (John 10:10). This promise is like the open sky above us, and it is only as we dare to go higher that we will start to see the possibilities beyond our old horizons.

The Life You Were Set Free For

Jesus had a disciple called John who in turn had a disciple called Polycarp and Polycarp had a disciple called Irenaeus. In about 180AD, Irenaeus wrote these words:

"Jesus Christ, by His transcendent love, became as we are in order to make us as He is."[1]

Three generations after Jesus' earthly life, His Church still be-lieved that He had come to give them the kind of life that He Himself had lived. Sadly, in the millennium that followed, Jesus' Church gradually relegated the "abundant life" to the "after-life". Being a follower of Jesus meant believing the right things, keeping the right rules and being in the right church.

However, the good news is that over the last 500 years, Jesus has been restoring lost truth to His Church. Our faith is not, and was never meant to be, just "pie in the sky when you die". Abun-dant life in Christ Jesus is not boring - it is an adventure and a challenge. It is a life lived in connection with heaven by the Holy Spirit; a journey into the fullness of God's favour, supernatural encounters and spiritual authority. It is a life naturally and easily connected to meaning and purpose. It may be painful and costly at times, but it is the most satisfying life you can ever live. It is life in full *technicolour* and once tasted it is addictive. It is what I call the "*supra*-natural" life! In other words, the life we were made for and for which we were set free!

Participating in the Divine

"His divine power has provided everything that enables life and holiness by the means of fully knowing Him who called us to glory and excellence. By this means we are given the biggest and most precious promises: That by these you become participators of the divine nature" (2 Peter 1:2-4a)

This series of books is about how we participate in Jesus' divine nature. It is about how to press in to the life and holiness that fully knowing Jesus and His divine power enables in us. It is about the "abundant life" that Jesus modelled and promised to us. It is about having the life and holiness that Jesus had and for which He endured the cross so that you could have it too.

Why "Supra-natural"?

'"Supra" is a prefix that describes going *above and beyond the usual.*

In attempting to communicate its meaning, I used to use the term "the naturally-supernatural, normal Christian life" - a reference to Watchmen Nee's famous book on discipleship[2], but it was a bit of a mouthful. I needed something punchier and more memorable. The word *supernatural* seemed too narrow and overused. Of course, the *supra*-natural life includes the supernatural: words of knowledge, healings, miracles etc. But the word supernatural doesn't capture the full experience of life connected to heaven that I want to explore in these books. And so I have coined the phrase "supra-natural".

Supra-natural living is experiencing the flavour of favour. It is the hallmark of blessing on a life that is fully connected to the purposes and values of a good Father God. It means that all the natural aspects of life - working, playing, relating, developing, ageing, parenting and so on - get done with heaven's help in a way that is beyond what is normal without it.

The supra-natural life that Jesus has for us cannot be understood just in terms of the life we have led so far. It requires an inner transformation that changes everything, but that still leaves the essential you and me intact. If we just pursue a bigger, slicker version of who we are today, or if we try to emulate one of our heroes in the faith, we will never be who we were made to be. The journey into the supra-natural life requires us to cross borders into unfamiliar territories. As we pass from glory to glory we find that whole new ways of being, thinking and experiencing are opening up to us.

This series is written for those who are prepared for the lifetime adventure of the upward call of God. We will explore what it really means to be human in the way that Jesus modelled it. We will look at the general purpose and calling of all disciples. But we will also see how the Father specifically calls and anoints each one of us, turning our life from a series of half-planned and accidental events into a redemptive story with real meaning and purpose. We will all learn to hear Jesus more clearly, both over time and in the moment, so that we know how to act and behave. We will learn how to nurture and weigh prophecy so that it can carry out its creative work in us. We will learn to feel and cooperate with the Holy Spirit and understand better how to exercise faith without presumption. We will learn how to grow spiritual fruit, how to use spiritual gifts and how to see and think from heaven's perspective.

These books are written to facilitate fresh Holy Spirit revelation as you read them. On it's own, information puffs us up, but revelation transforms us. But of course, information can be the seed for revelation if we let the Holy Spirit get hold of it. So as you read through these books you will discover there are places where I ask you to pray and hear back from Jesus; to reflect and remember and write things down as He talks to you. There are things to try out and discussions to be had. You don't have to do all the exercises, but you will get more out of these books if you do.

The life Jesus died to give you is a life full of colour - a supranatural life. The thought of you living life this way was part of the joy Jesus anticipated as He faced the cross (Hebrews 12:2). Fulfilling your destiny is the reward for His suffering. So jump in. Live your earthly life like this from now on! Don't hang around waiting for eternity!

You were created to live like an eagle. Don't settle for being the biggest pigeon in the park.

Endnotes:

1. Preface of "Against Heresies" Book V, by Irenaeus.

2. *The Normal Christian Life* by Watchman Nee

Introduction

You have a destiny! But your destiny is less about the things you are supposed to do in life, as it is about the life you are supposed to do things with.

You have an inheritance in Jesus. But it is not an inheritance that you will automatically claim in this life and, sadly, a vast number of those who follow Jesus don't. However, the tide seems to be turning. It seems that every year more and more Christians *are* discovering the truth of what it is to live the supra-natural life.

The moment we are saved, we metaphorically cross the Red Sea and are externally free from the slavery of Egypt forever. But Egypt's grip on our inner lives is harder to shift. Between ourselves and the inheritance Jesus has for us there is a wilderness. The journey across this wilderness is not instantaneous. For the Israelites it was a journey that could have taken less than a month, but in the end took forty years, resulting in just one person in a million actually crossing the Jordan and making it into a land flowing with blessing.

It took just days to get out of Egypt, but it can take a lifetime to get Egypt out of us!

This book is about is about how to be changed by the journey out of slavery to be ready for Canaan.

When I was 16 a man called Harry Sprange prophesied a prophetic ministry over my life. As a teenager I would imagine what
this might look like. I used to imagine myself at public landmarks,
wild eyed and dramatic, long hair blowing in the wind, or on TV
debates railing against the evils in our nation with insight and
passion.

The first obstacle to me achieving my expectation of Jesus' calling was the early onset of male pattern baldness. My hair may
have been blowing in the wind, but unfortunately it wasn't stuck
to my head! A more serious obstacle to me being what I thought
a prophet should be was that I didn't really hear Jesus very clearly.
For many years the idea of me having a prophetic call seemed so
unlikely I had stopped even trying to realise it. I became comfortable in telling people that I didn't really hear God in the moment,
just over time with lots of thinking and meditation.

Today, I operate in a prophetic ministry, but it looks nothing
like I imagined it would all those years ago. I've discovered that
Jesus was telling the truth when He said, *"My sheep hear my voice"*
(John 10:27). Everyone can learn to hear Jesus. Even when we
don't understand what He's saying, His words can still calm us,
guide us and change us.

Nevertheless, my history in this area means that I am still surprised when someone confirms the details of a word I have given
to them.

But here's the thing: prophesying is now as natural to me as
praying and prayer is as natural to me as breathing. I hardly have a
private thought these days - they are all part of a dialogue with Father and Jesus. From good deals in the supermarket to my desire to
see a sick person healed, every moment of life has the possibility to
transcend the normal - but in the most natural way, because Jesus
does speak to me, the Spirit does lead me and Father really loves
me. The same is true for us all! The tragedy is that we can miss
out on the incredible life Jesus has for us because we have tried

living according to our pre-conceptions of what our lives should be. When it doesn't make sense or doesn't work, we think we have failed and then we give up. The supra-natural life is actually very natural. It is not something we achieve in ourselves , or strive to be successful in, it happens as our nature is changed, as the old version of us is taken off and the new version is put on (Ephesians 4:22-24).

Supra-natural Life 101

This book is about the general process of personal transformation and growth, and it's ultimate goal. A process that takes us from who we are naturally (shaped by our personal history, DNA and choices), into who we are prophetically (re-shaped by revelation, redemption and cooperation), until Christ is formed in us (Galatians 4:19).

Our transformation in this life seems to be one of the major themes in the New Testament. It is full of encouragements for us to grow into the *"full measure of Christ"* (Ephesians 4:13); to be *"changed from glory to glory"* (2 Corinthians 3:18); to *"be renewed in knowledge according to the image of our creator"* (Colossians 3:10); to *"be transformed by the renewing of our minds"* (Romans 12:2) ... and so on.

In this book you will find testimony stories of healings, words of knowledge, accounts of super-natural provision, miracles and favour. These are all the fruit of the supra-natural life.

"The blessed man ... Is a tree planted by waters ... with green leaves ... and even in years of drought, they continue to produce fruit." (Jeremiah 17:7-8)

So as well as stories of fruit, this book will explore how to draw on the life-giving waters of the Holy Spirit and words of grace. These are the roots of the supra-natural life. And it will look at how to cooperate with the Holy Spirit to produce growth, strength and transformation, which are the shoots that produce the fruit. Simply trying to do the same things you read in the stories will not produce the life in you that produces fruit naturally.

In many ways this is a book of two halves. The first half looks at the foundations and theory of the supra-natural life: the roots. The second half focuses on the practices of the supra-natural life which produce shoots in us.

The key to fruits is a life with roots and shoots!

It is the Holy Spirit's work to transform us from glory to glory (2 Corinthians 3:18), but both experience and Scripture are quite clear that we can cooperate with His work in us or we can fight against it - or perhaps most commonly we simply miss and undermine what He is doing.

It seems that every now and again we get a glimpse of what this transformed life could look like, but mostly our faith is a set of propositions to be believed - a helpful set of ideas and principles through which to see the world. We eagerly adopt various useful self-help tools and are helped along by our church community to whom we feel connected as we journey through life. But life's journey should be a *pilgrimage*. A pilgrimage, by definition, has an objective, a place to get to. It has purpose and intent. It changes the pilgrim as he or she travels. This book could just be another set of things to believe in, a manual of new self-improvement principles. But I have not written it for that reason. My prayer is that that it encourages and guides you on your spiritual journey in a different way.

I Know This Works!

I feel able to write this book not because I am an expert (I wish I were further ahead than I currently am), but because I have been stuck in a rut as a professional Christian so often, found it deeply dissatisfying, cried out for more, and so have been forced to consciously learn what needs to change.

Wonderfully, what I have found is that the lessons I have learned and continue to learn have been helpful to others too. It has been a great delight while leading River Church to see incredible transformations in individuals, some of whom had been Christians for years, but had got stuck in religious routines.

Today, River Church is a charismatic church not only in name, but in practice with lots of people walking in more of their giftings, ministries and callings.

Take Oliver. Oliver wasn't brought up as a Christian but got saved into what Jesus has been doing with us over the last few years. Oliver was in town and went to buy a copy of the "Big Issue", the magazine sold by those who are homeless. The lady selling the magazine had a bandage on her hand so he asked if he could pray for her. She agreed and after he had prayed she started shaking her whole arm saying, "The pain in my arm has gone!" Oliver had only known about the sprained hand because he saw the bandage, but Jesus had gone beyond what he asked for.

Then there's Louise, Hannah and Tim. One day they went out "treasure hunting" (a practice we learnt from Bethel Church in Redding, California). They each asked the Lord for a word that would help them connect with someone they would meet. The three words they received were "hairdressers", "blue" and the name "Emma". They wrote the words down and went out to meet people to offer prayers and blessings. Towards the end of their time they noticed a hairdressers tucked away down a side street with a blue front, so they went in. A girl approached them and greeted them with "Hello, I'm Emma. How can I help?" They showed her their piece of paper and explained how Jesus loved her enough to send them. Then they prayed for her and left.

On another occasion, a girl collecting for charity approached my friend Dave in a shopping precinct. Prompted by the story of the lame man at the temple he told her "I'm afraid I haven't got any change, but can offer you prayer for healing or a spiritual reading." The girl became interested and asked to know more, so Dave explained: "I'm a Christian and if you like I can pray for you if you need anything or I can ask God to show me something for you." The girl became defensive and cynical at this. It seemed she had some bad experience of church and Christians, so as she backed off she replied, "Oh yeah? Well if God talks to you He can tell you my name!" Dave sent up a quick prayer and said, "Well, it doesn't usually work like that, but the name in my head right now is 'Emily'" The girl, who was called Emily, nearly fell over. Dave went on to explain how much Jesus loved her and he prayed with her.

I could go on telling stories like this. I hear them regularly from people in River Church, which is how I know that the lessons in this book, if understood and implemented, can release the supra-natural life. But I also know that they will not be everything you will need. The supra-natural life is *caught* more than it is *taught*, so one of the best things you can do for yourself is to make sure you are in a church community that is really serious about growing in Jesus.

And remember that God, *"...is able to do exceedingly beyond what we ask or think, according to the power that works within us"* (Ephesians 3:20)

1: The Horizon Ahead

"...to those who love God, who are called with a purpose,
*concerning whom he knew beforehand he had also **pre-planned***
***to be conformed to the image of His Son**, so that He would be the*
first born in a big family."
(Romans 8:28b-29)[1]

If you love God you have a calling and purpose! That calling and purpose will look different for each of us. However, at another level it always requires us to become just like Jesus. "To be conformed to the image of His Son" is the Father's foreknown, pre-planned destiny for you.

Being conformed to the image of Jesus is about you becoming who Jesus would have been if He had been born into your family with your DNA, had experienced your childhood and was now living your life to its supra-natural potential.

In Greek, the word that I have translated "pre-planned" in the verse above is made up of two parts: "pro" which means "before" or "for" something and "orizo" which is a line or boundary. God's plan for you is not a narrow path that runs from where we are now far into the distance. It is more like a marker or target line ahead of us. In English, *orizo* gives us the word "horizon". So a loose translation of this verse could be:

"He has set a horizon before us, to be conformed to the image of his Son."

For me, this conveys some of the feel and real meaning of the verse that is lost in some translations.

Wherever you are in your pilgrimage with Jesus, the Father is pointing you towards a distant skyline where Christ is fully formed in you. He is calling you to an adventure of faith, to walk an undiscovered path towards a broad horizon. Your standard is not the person next to you or even a hero in the faith. The horizon ahead of us is the ascended Jesus.

"For as he is, so are we in this world" (1 John 4:17b)

How Far is the Journey?

As I read the gospels I often find stories which reflect experiences that I have had or seen first hand. I have seen large numbers of people being healed in one place, deliverances, weather miracles, the supernatural provision of money to pay my taxes and so on, but there are also things that go beyond my experience, such as walking on water and raising the dead that I have not yet personally seen. Jesus did all these things in His earthly life.

After His resurrection Jesus walked through walls and was spiritually transported from place to place. Philip the Evangelist proved that this type of travel is an experience that belongs to the Christian life when it happened to him (Acts 8:39-40). Transport in the spirit is not something I have experienced, but I know several people who have and one day I expect to too.

But Jesus went further. Beyond His resurrection He ascended and sat down at the right hand of His Father and received all authority both in heaven and on earth.

Interestingly, Paul had only ever seen and met the ascended Jesus, so it is the ascended Jesus that Paul has in mind when he says it is our destiny to become just like Him!

That is the thing about a horizon. As you walk towards it you start to see beyond what you initially saw. So even when every part of your life has been redeemed and shaped in the image of Jesus as you have known Him, there will always be a deeper revelation of who He is to draw you further.

I do understand if it feels hard to believe that you could be like the ascended Jesus. Sometimes I feel that way too. But I've also learned that these feelings don't have to be the measure or limits of my faith. They are just the environment in which I have to find and exercise faith that takes me beyond what I ask or think. By faith we can overcome the limits of our understanding and each mini-step of faith will build, *"precept on precept, precept on precept; line on line, line on line; a little here, a little there"* (Isaiah 28:10). Before long you will realise you have come a long way and the original horizon, while still far off, will seem more attainable and we will be seeing beyond the old limits. There will be new challenges and revelation, new borders to cross and a new panorama to be inspired by.

So when it comes to being conformed to Jesus' image, any limit I might impose is not based on Scripture. Romans chapter eight is all about our transformation in this life, and the target it sets is the ascended Jesus, even if we don't fully see all that that means just yet.

He is the horizon set before us!

The Son of Man

"What is man, that you are mindful of him? What is the son of man that you care for him?" (Psalm 8:4)

Jesus, of course, loved to emphasise that He was the "Son of Man". It was His favourite title or way of describing Himself and He used it over eighty times in the Gospels. When Jesus originally said it in Aramaic He would have actually said, "Son of Adam".

It was like Jesus was calling Himself "Joe Human". He was saying, "I am everyman". It was a title, but it was also a way for Jesus to emphasise that all that He did, all that He said and all that He knew, had been accomplished as a man, living a human life, not as we know it, but as it was supposed to be lived.

So What is Man?

Man is a unique alloy of the dirt of this world with the breath of heaven.

"The Lord God formed man from the dust of the ground, and breathed into his nostrils the breath of life; and man became a living soul." (Genesis 2:7)

Man combined an earthy heritage with a divine impartation and this tension made Man unique. He wasn't an angel, although like them he was a son of God. He wasn't an animal, though he shared their biology and chemistry. Man was the joining point of heaven to creation. Man was always made to live in and out of both the flesh (his "earthiness") and the spirit (his "heavenliness"). It was not an either/or situation, it was a question of priority. We were made to live *out of* the spirit[2], but *through* the flesh.[3]

Psalm 115 tells us,

"The heavens are the heavens of the Lord, but the earth he has given to the children of men." (Psalm 115:16)

Earth was God's gift to mankind in creation. Both male and female were given authority over all the earth, all animal and plant life.

*"And God said, Let's make mankind in our image, after our likeness: and **let them have dominion** over the fish of the sea, and over the birds of the air, and over the cattle, and **over all the earth,** and over every creeping thing that creeps upon the earth. So God created mankind in His own image, in the image of God He created him; male and female He created them."* (Genesis 1:26-27)

God made us in His image so that He could extend the love He already had within His own triune being to include us. Furthermore, to make us in His image required that we had a sphere to exercise our God-likeness in. So God gave mankind an authority on earth, and what He gives He doesn't take away (Romans 11:29), though of course, that doesn't stop us losing it.

Adam gave control away to the devil. As the mess had been made on earth, it was man's responsibility to clean it up. If God had simply fixed it all as God, it would have taken something away from humanity. Mankind would no longer be what we were made to be and essentially the whole human project would have been a failure.

This is why Jesus had to come in the flesh *as a man* to fix earth's problems *as a man* and in doing so, taking mankind from defeat into victory.

The Father's original commission still stands. We are supposed to have dominion on earth in a way that reflects the purposes of heaven. This is true even though our separation from God's presence severely handicaps our ability to do this. But, of course, that separation was exactly what Jesus came as a man to fix.

When Jesus taught us to pray, *"Your will be done on earth as it is in heaven"* (Matthew 6:10, Luke 11:2), He was inviting us to live the way we were always supposed to, making us participants or agents in expressing the kingship of heaven to earth. We can do that because the human soul, the deepest or highest point of creation, is the joining place of heaven and earth. It is the place where heaven's plans and purposes are supposed to infuse earthly authority, to be released into creation through our flesh. As the arch-type of what man should be, as the Son of Man, Jesus modelled the way our authority was to work.

As the Son of Man, Jesus lived a complete human life from the cradle to the grave and beyond. He did it in such a victorious way that it lifted the whole human project out of failure and into success.

The supra-natural life is one that expresses the victory of Jesus in us, and is lived in and by the Holy Spirit.

In the next chapter we will look in much more detail at just how Jesus lived His life so supra-naturally. But for now it is important to note that what was initiated in heaven was completed by Jesus using His flesh.[4] The flesh is not intrinsically evil, without it we would not be human. It is simply that our flesh is supposed to be fully subject to our spirits, which are supposed to be listening to heaven.

When we use our flesh to do something that has been initiated in or by the Holy Spirit we call it an "act of faith". Acts of faith release the purposes of heaven onto the earth. They are also the bread and butter activity of the supra-natural life and faith is the mark of a righteous life.

The "Right" Life of Faith

To live righteously is not about doing the right thing, it is about living the right way!

"...that no one is justified by the Law in the sight of God is clear, for, 'The righteous shall live by faith.'" (Galatians 3:11)

There is a joke which serves a point.

A man gets a new job as a lumberjack. On the first day he is given his equipment and told he can work as he likes, but his target is to fell twenty trees in a day. At the end of the first day he returns hot and sweaty, but has only managed five trees. The foreman is concerned but recognises it's his first day and so just encourages him to do better tomorrow. The next day the man returns with cuts and shredded clothing, exhausted by the day's labour, but he has still only managed to cut down ten trees. The foreman doesn't want to fire him as he's obviously trying hard, so offers to take him out and show him how to cut down a tree efficiently. At the forest, the foreman puts on his gloves, hardhat and protective goggles, picks up the chainsaw and fires it up. At which point the new employee jumps and cries out surprised, "What's that noise!?"

Possibly not the world's funniest joke, but it helps me make my point. Last Christmas, my mother-in-law gave me an electric chainsaw. The thing has vicious teeth and I have already almost lost a finger and fallen out of a eucalyptus tree whilst swinging it wildly. I could use the chainsaw to cut down branches by pulling and pushing it manually (like the man in the joke in case you missed that!) or I could plug it in and let it slice. The box says that cutting branches is what it is made for, so I would be "doing the right thing" with it, though I would be doing it the wrong way! As the songs says: **"It ain't what ya' do, it's the way that ya' do it."**

Faith is the right way to do it. Sometimes people use the word "faith" to mean "believing in something impossible" or "believing in something without evidence", but neither of these are what the Bible calls faith. In Scripture, faith is *the expression, in action or words, of an idea or instruction that has been initiated in heaven.* That is why *"faith comes by hearing and hearing by the word of God"* (Romans 10:17). As James points out, faith is completed by an action (James 2:22), but it is an action that expresses a word heard from heaven that releases a power way beyond the ability of the do-er.

The Bible says that there is no set of rules that we can follow that will make us righteous (Galatians 3:21), but that the hope (or goal) of righteousness is attained through the Spirit by faith (Galatians 5:5). In other words, you are righteous because your faith is acting out of the leading of the Holy Spirit. We will explore the details and dynamics of living by faith more fully in the third book in this series, but for this book it is important to see that faith is the fruit of listening to what heaven speaks to us, and it is the means by which heaven's purposes are released through the things we do.

Jesus' actions healed the sick, broke the bonds of the demonic, calmed storms, fed thousands from a single packed lunch or kept the party going with new wine. He did all this as "Joe Human" in proper relationship with his heavenly Father, **living from the Spirit but through His flesh.**

"...I do nothing on my own initiative, but as the Father taught me I speak ... and I always do the things that are pleasing to Him!" (John 8:28-29)

This was true too for His greatest feat, achieving salvation and redemption for the whole world. On the cross, through the submission of His flesh to the purposes of heaven, *"not my will, but yours"* (Luke 22:42), *"He condemned sin **in the flesh**"* (Romans 8:3). His mission, which was initiated in heaven, was implemented and completed through His flesh **by an act of faith.**

The More Than Normal Christian Life

The cross, of course, was a unique event. It was the one thing that Jesus did which required Him to be both the eternal Son of God and the temporal Son of Man. But absolutely everything else He did stands as an example to inspire us in what we can be.

"Certainly I tell you, whoever believes in me they will do the works I do as well; and they will do greater works than these, because I am going to my Father..." (John 14:12)

We can walk in more favour and authority than Jesus walked in during His earthly life because it is His resurrected and ascended life that lives in us and Jesus is committed to releasing that life by our transformation. The only limit is the level and extent of our cooperation. And cooperation is often dependent on expectation.

In my head, I had always believed Jesus' words about His followers doing more than He did, but I believed them through the filter of my heart's expectation. To me they meant that some Christians had things happen to them that could be considered "bigger" miracles than are recorded in the Gospels. I had both heard about and actually met people with remarkable miracle stories. My own testimony included a dramatic healing and I spoke in tongues and prayed for the sick and sometimes people got better. The trouble was, I suppose, that I tended to think that supernatural incidents where the icing on the cake of what is the "normal" Christian life. You know the life I mean? You do good, forgive those around you, talk to Jesus about the things you want and need, you witness a bit, give money to good causes, you hear of or see the odd healing and you feel the gentle nudging of the Holy Spirit over time as you seek guidance.

My life was being spent on a worthy cause, but it was a cake of very normal ingredients with just enough icing and sprinkles of divine intervention to make it interesting.

Today I am discovering a totally different life - one where miracles and revelation are a weekly and often daily occurrence. I experience the tangible presence of God and dialogue with Him throughout the day and probably no one is more surprised at this than me.

What I used to think of as "icing" is actually a main ingredient in the cake that is the supra-natural life. And the more I get used to living off this cake, the more the possibilities of *"life in Christ Jesus"* (Romans 8:2) open up before me.

This is the life for which Jesus took hold of me (Philippians 3:12). This is the life for which Jesus endured the cross. This is the type of life I should expect as I head for the horizon while Christ is being formed in me (Galatians 4:19).

Let me tell you about the last 10 days.[5]

Yesterday, my friend Dave and I went to minister at a Baptist church in London. As people came in, I saw an older lady walking with a stick. She looked happy, but I could see that she had had a tough life and in my spirit I felt drawn to her, so I went over and started chatting. She told me her wonderful testimony of meeting Jesus, how her youngest daughter had started coming to church, and how then she had come along too because her daughter had been so much happier. It was at that point in her life that she had met Jesus.

I asked about her stick. She explained she had fallen a few months before and broken some ribs and her right arm was now locked up. However, the main reason she needed the stick was because of long-term sciatica and osteoarthritis. While people were still arriving for the meeting I asked if I could pray for her. I got her to stand up and laid hands on her and released healing to her. Her whole body rippled and she staggered backwards into her chair saying, "Oh my goodness, oh my goodness!" I asked her how her arm was and she lifted it above her head. I asked what she had felt in her side and leg. "I can't feel anything," she said. "Do you mean nothing has happened yet?" I asked. "No, I mean I can't feel any pain," she replied. The next Sunday she danced at the front of church to demonstrate what Jesus had done for her.

After the meeting (at which two more people received instant healing), I was praying for a lady called Linda. I felt I should ask if her husband was there and he was, so he was brought over. I knew the Lord wanted to say something and as I prayed I just said what I "saw".

"Andy, I see you in a shed doing a hobby. The Lord is taking you out of the shed with your hobby into a wider group, but it's not the Church. He is giving you relationships with people who share your interest and you will not have to try hard at communicating."

Then for Linda I prayed, "Linda I see you writing. You used to think you were not a good writer at school, but this is not about technique. You have a message so you need to write. Maybe you just start writing for the church newsletter, but it won't stop there..."

Afterwards, they told me that Linda edited the church magazine and Andy's hobby was audio and video. He did indeed have a shed where he edited sound and video files for the church website and he had recently joined the local video and film-making club, making new relationships with people who shared his interest.

At one level, neither of these "words" were particularly life-changing, but they were life-affirming and deeply encouraged this couple that the Lord cared enough about their interests to speak about them.

A similar thing had happened the weekend before when I had been at a leaders' gathering. Praying for a lady I hardly knew, I used the phrase, "You have learnt to speak with your hands". I was thinking it referred to "acts of service", but she told me afterwards that over the previous eighteen months she had learnt sign language for use in her ministry with children.

Then with another leader I "saw" him "looking into a derelict shop with dreams in his heart". He then told me how he and his youth pastor had stood outside a derelict shop just that week, discussing whether they could start a youth work in it.

In between these two meetings there were too many examples of God's intervention to mention: trivial provisions, encouragements, words of wisdom for pastoral situations and so on. Actually, none of them are really trivial, they are the love languages the Father uses that give us the courage to step out and take risks, to live a supra-natural life.

In the middle of the 10-day period I've just described I stepped out with a "word of knowledge" for a shop assistant. The trouble is that it was a word of presumption rather than a word of knowledge and turned out to be wrong. There was a moment of awkward silence as I asked her something odd. I had crossed a line in customer-sales assistant etiquette, but that was all. I went away smiling, glad I'd had the courage to step out, even though it didn't work. In the past I would not have done this unless I was "on an outreach" and had psyched myself up for some scary encounters with non-Christians so that I would have something to report back. I now know that I don't need to be right to be loved by my Father; I don't need to perform to feel valued. And as for the sales lady, she may just have thought I was trying to flirt with her unsuccessfully!

None of the incidents I have just described can really be called a "greater work" than the things that Jesus did. But they are given as examples of the fruit of life lived the way that Jesus modelled for us and which the Bible tells us was the way we were always meant to live. This is life in the Spirit.

In the next chapter we will look at the how Jesus cooperated with the Holy Spirit and listened for heaven's instructions and we will think about what it meant for Jesus to grow into maturity. Then the rest of this book will explore how to follow Jesus' example to experience the type of personal growth He went through as preparation for a life of miracles. Later books in the series will explore the practice of the miraculous in more depth.

But first, I want to tell you a story that inspires me to keep pushing for more, for the greater works.

It happened to a man called Bill Turner who used to come and minister in my parents' church. Bill has some incredible stories from his walk with Jesus over nearly 80 years, ones that were easy to disbelieve until you met him. Bill was the real deal, a man who lived with a passion for the life he had in Jesus. One day he was walking down a hill in his hometown when he met a man, George, who he had known at school. Bill asked how he was doing and George told him, "Not well at all. I've had two heart operations and I need another. It's scheduled for a couple of week's time." Bill offered to pray for him, so they stepped into the doorway of a men's clothing store, to stand out of the drizzle. Bill prayed for George and they left each other.

A few weeks later, Bill was talking with his brother, Tom, and another friend, Albert and he mentioned that he had met George. Albert already knew this, as George had written to him to tell him how he had met Bill at the bottom of the hill in Hastings, a town on the South coast of England, how they had stepped into a doorway of a shop called "Greenwoods" and how afterwards he had been completely healed and had run back up the hill. This was all just as Bill remembered it, except that for Bill it had happened 200 miles away near his hometown of Stoke-on-Trent, in the Midlands, and the shop was "Dennison's Gentleman's Outfitters".

Bill called the experience "bi-location". It is not a miracle that we know about in Scripture, though of course it could have happened and the two parties not known about it. But it is not too different from Philip's experience (Acts 8:39) or Ezekiel's finding himself in the Temple in Jerusalem while he was praying in Babylon. For me it's a great example of the "beyond what we ask or think" that we are told to expect if the power of God is working in us (Ephesians 3:20). You see, Bill wasn't trying to achieve this miracle, but he was always looking for the Holy Spirit's connection and leading in life, which is how we're supposed to live, and then these things happen.

Before Proceeding...

The next chapter is going to look at what humanity looked like in Jesus. Later chapters are more practical. But even when a chapter is more explanation than application, it can be used to inspire a dialogue with Jesus.

Throughout this book there will be exercises, things to do. If you do them I guarantee you will get so much more long-term benefit from this book - and if you've paid good money to buy it, it makes sense to maximise the benefit of your investment!

The foundation of the supra-natural life is to be constantly tuned to the presence of God and to His Holy Spirit. It is the simple discipline of processing life with Him. So as you read each question, take some moments to quieten yourself, ask the Lord to give you the mind of Christ, or to have ears to hear, then put the questions to the Holy Spirit, not just to your own head. Give some space to "hear" something back. Don't worry too much as to whether what you hear has come from you or the Holy Spirit. Write down any impressions, words or thoughts, or even pictures you have. As you write the answers down, stay engaged with God to see if you get further clarity or new thoughts.

So before we storm the next chapter, try some or all of the following.

---

1. Look up all the Bible verses quoted in this chapter and highlight them in your Bible in a way that will remind you in the years to come that these verses have something to say about your transformation.

2. Now use the blank space between this chapter and the next, or your prayer journal to answer the following questions:

> a. What do you want to get out of this book?
> b. What are the specific areas of your life that you know you want to see breakthrough in?
> c. What have been the highlights of your Christian life so far?

3. Now tell Jesus and Father your answers to question 2, asking if He has anything to say to you about these things. If you "hear", "feel" or "think" anything write it down. You can work out later whether it was from God or not.

4. Now go back through the chapter and write down the key points and the stand-alone phrases highlighted in bold. Writing them down will help you remember them and these sound-bites will become a summary of what you will learn.

Endnotes:

1. I have used a version of this verse that avoids the more theologically loaded words such as "foreknew" and "predestined" because these words

have taken on special meanings that reflect the later impositions of theologians. In doing this they obscure the basic meaning of these verses by making them about the process of "election" rather than a statement about what God intended for those who love Him.

2. The fact that we have a human spirit, but as Christians we also have the Holy Spirit is often confusing. We will think about what it means to have the Holy Spirit in us in more detail later, but please note that when I write "spirit" I am focusing on the human spirit and when I write "Spirit" I mean the Holy Spirit, either "in" us or active "on" or "with" us.

3. The term "flesh" includes the concept of the soul if the soul is not submitted to the human spirit and the Holy Spirit.

4. The Apostle John points out that it was a dangerous heresy to deny Jesus' humanity, one that undermined the Gospel's power (1 John 4:2-3, 2 John 7). But while orthodox Christianity vigorously defends the doctrine that Jesus came in the flesh, it often forgets the implications of that truth.

5. This book has developed over time. As a result, when I use references such as, "last week" or "the last 10 days", they should be understood as being true when I originally wrote a particular section of text, not at the point the final editing happened. This might give the impression that I had an extremely busy month just before writing this book! But I wanted to keep the feel of freshness as this is part of the message of the book, the supra-natural life is something to be lived day by day, not debated on the basis of past experiences.

2: Truly, Newly, Human

Jesus didn't come so much to show us what God could do, as to show us what man could be!

*"So ... let's also lay aside every weight and sin that entangles us and let's run the race before us with endurance, focused on **Jesus the pioneer and highest example of faith**."* (Hebrews 12:1b-2a)

Faith is the way that the righteous live and Jesus was the exemplary righteous man. His life wrote the manual on how to do it. However, Jesus did more than just show us *what* we could be, He also showed us *how to be it* and then, in His death, resurrection and ascension, He gave us the tools and tokens of office that we require to live the role He calls us to.

There is so much we can learn from the life of Jesus once we have realised that He lived within the same limitations that we do. But for the purposes of this book I want to focus on just three main truths from which we can draw principles to live our own lives by.

First: Jesus was constantly **tuned into and aware of the Holy Spirit** in many different ways.

Second: Jesus grew into maturity, it was not something He was born with, neither did it suddenly happen to Him.

Third: Jesus lived by the words He heard from heaven.

Jesus lived a fully human life as the Son of Man and we shall

think about what it now means for us to have a share in His successful life by the deposit of His Spirit that He has given each one
of us.

*"The first Adam became a living soul. The last Adam became a life
giving spirit."* (1 Corinthians 15:45)

Jesus was truly human. The Bible calls him the last Adam, but
the way Jesus did "human" was new. In practice, at least, **Jesus
was truly, newly human**. So by putting His Spirit within us He
has sown into us the seeds of a whole new type of humanity. The
Spirit that He has put *in us* has a distinct and different role to the
Spirit that comes *on us* or the Spirit as He works *with us*. The Spirit
that comes *on us* is often the more dramatic in its manifestation,
but the Spirit that He puts *in us* cost more to give. It required the
death and resurrection of Jesus. It is the Spirit *in us* that makes us
a new creation and partners in His divine nature. But we still need
to cooperate with the Spirit *on us* and *with us* if we are going to live
the right (or righteous) way.

Life Born of the Spirit

*"The wind blows where it wills, you hear its sound, but don't know
where it comes from and where it is going. So is everyone who is born
of the Spirit."* (John 3:8)

Jesus says these words to Nicodemus just after famously telling him he *"must be born again"*. Actually, Jesus doesn't say *"born
again"*. Technically He says *"born from above"*.[1] This may seem like
a semantic point, but it's important because according to Jesus, to
be *"born again"* is to be *"born of the Spirit"* and Jesus was *"born of
the Spirit"* from conception. So Jesus was *"born again"*, but before
He was born naturally, which is why it is better to say He was
"born from above".

So, like us, Jesus was born both naturally and supernaturally.
The only difference between Jesus and us is the order in which

these two births happened. Jesus was *"born from above"* before He had been *"born of water"*.

"Most certainly I tell you, unless one is born of water² and spirit, he can't enter into the Kingdom of God! That which is born of the flesh is flesh. That which is born of the Spirit is spirit." (John 3:5-6)

I have a friend, Colin, who is very particular about the way he makes his cups of tea. He tells me that you can taste the difference if you add the milk to the cup *after* you pour in the tea (this is the heretical post-lactarian practice), rather than the other way around (real tea connoisseurs' prefer the pre-lactarian orthodoxy). But in the end, whether the tea goes in the cup before the milk or vice-versa, you still have a cup of tea with milk. Unless, like me, you're a-lactarian and your tea has a nice slice of lemon!

Our lives may have a slightly different flavour to Jesus' due to the fact that the Spirit got put into our cup after we had accumulated some history in the flesh. But fundamentally, once we got saved our life contained the same basic ingredients that Jesus' life had as the "Son of Man". A human can't come into God's purposes for themselves without being born in both of these ways and because Jesus was fully human this was as true for Him as it is for us.

Man was made to be the interface between Creator and creation, between time and eternity, between heaven and earth. To be this, he must carry within himself something of the divine nature as well as having an earthly component. In the begining man is made from the same stuff as the rest of creation is made from, but it was when the breath of God came into him that he became a living soul (Genesis 2:7).

At the end of John's Gospel, Jesus breathes onto His disciples and says, *"Receive the Holy Spirit"* (John 20:22). This soul-refreshing breeze is the moment of regeneration - the moment you are *"born from above"*. It is a clear re-enactment of the Genesis account of creation. Jesus is inaugurating a new type of humanity. You are a new creation! (2 Corinthians 5:17).

You are made of mud and glory!

This second divine impartation was better than the first. In simple terms it is because the Spirit of God now has a part of Himself that is fully human. It is as though the Holy Spirit can now be breathed into us in a new and deeper way without compromising our humanness because it has now lived a full human life in Jesus. John is quite explicit in his gospel that the Holy Spirit had not been fully given to live permanently in the disciples while Jesus was on earth, because Jesus had not yet died and been raised (John 7:39; 14:17).

If Jesus was truly, newly human from birth, we are newly truly human from the moment we get saved!

It is important to really let this fact sink in. We are fundamentally different once we have received the life-giving Spirit of Jesus. So many try to live the life Jesus calls them to as if it was just a fresh attempt at what they had failed at the first time. But the supranatural life can't be lived by our old nature. Our nature changed when we where born from above and the Spirit came into us.

Three Dimensions of the Holy Spirit in Jesus' Life

Jesus wasn't just born of the Spirit. At His baptism in water, the Holy Spirit comes *on* Jesus and remains in a new way (John 1:32). And during His ministry Jesus seems to have taught His disciples how to cooperate with the Holy Spirit who was *with*[3] them.

*"The Spirit of truth, whom the world can't receive; because they neither perceive him, nor know him, you know him because he lives **with** you, but will be **in** you."* (John 14:17)

Presumably, Jesus had lived a life even before His baptism which was marked out by the Spirit *with* Him (Luke 2:47). Likewise, He expected that the disciples were having this experience of the Holy Spirit before the day of Pentecost, so it is not unreasonable to believe that the Spirit was *with* Jesus as a child as well as being *in* Him from birth. Although we don't know much about Jesus' childhood, we do read that He was becoming strong in spirit and that God's grace was on Him (Luke 2:40).

In reality, of course, the Spirit in us, on us and with us is all the same Holy Spirit, so we shouldn't try to categorise or divide up His activity too neatly.[4] But to help our understanding it is helpful to think in these three dimensions:

The Spirit in us: is what connects us to heaven. It creates in us a permanent and unbreakable link to our Creator. It is the means by which our inner life is changed. It is the Spirit in us that potentially enables us to be who we were made to be. **The Spirit in us transforms the heart.**

The Spirit with us: is the way in which we know the Holy Spirit's cooperation to change and affect the world around us. Jesus knew *"the power of the Lord was with him to heal them"* (Luke 5:17). It is the Spirit with us who carries the consequences of our faith actions way beyond their natural impact zone. **The Spirit with us empowers the hand.**

The Spirit on us: is the way in which we receive our specific commission and anointing. It is the revealer of the truth of who we are. It is the Spirit on us that potentially empowers us to step into the fullness of our identity. **The Spirit on us anoints the head.**

Jesus was a man familiar with the Holy Spirit in all three dimensions. His engagement with the Holy Spirit was not a one-off nor a twice-only experience, it was an on-going, multi-dimensional, many-layered relationship.

- First Jesus was *conceived* by the Holy Spirit (Matthew 1:20)
- Then we read that He *grew strong* in spirit (Luke 2:40)[5]
- Then the Holy Spirit *came on* Jesus and opened up heaven for Him (Mark 1:10)
- Then Jesus, now *full of the Holy Spirit*, was *compelled* by the Holy Spirit into the wilderness (Mark 1:12; Luke 4:1)
- Then Jesus returns from the wilderness *in the power* of the Holy Spirit (Luke 4:14)

Or to put it another way:

Supra-natural activity is initiated by the Spirit in us, empowered by the Spirit with us and released by the Spirit on us.

On the cross, Jesus was to condemn sin *"in the flesh"* by the physical act of laying down His life for us. But Jesus' natural actions were never disconnected from the Spirit. He has already proclaimed *"it is finished"* before the Spirit left his body. Actually, the very last[6] word Jesus is to utter from the cross is the word *"Spirit"*.

"Father, into your hands I commit this[7] my Spirit" (Luke 23:46)

After crying out these words, all four gospels conclude by stating that Jesus gave up "the" or "his" Spirit.[8] When something occurs in all four gospels it is important.

I believe that in the death, resurrection and ascension of Jesus, something very profound is happening within the nature of God. Something that enables the Holy Spirit to live in us permanently without compromising our humanity. God is a creator and in this act He has created something new, both "under the sun" and within Himself. The Spirit of God now contains a fully-fledged and complete human spirit, one that has lived victoriously and righteously through every trial and battle of a full life.

People often find the concept of something changing in God difficult to accept, but Scripture has no problem with this idea.[9] Perhaps this particular change was the one thing that Jesus could accomplish, because He was the "Son of God", that a purely human person could not, because our sphere of authority is just the earth[10] and not heaven.

Therefore, nothing that Jesus accomplished in His natural life was done outside of the Spirit's embrace. **Jesus was conceived by the Spirit, He did life by the Spirit and the Spirit only left His body after He had said, "It is finished!"** (John 19:30).

Unfortunately, too many of Jesus' followers fall into the trap of doing some things with the Holy Spirit and others without Him. Paul's question to the Galatian church echoes through the ages:

"Are you so foolish? Having started by the Spirit are you going to be perfected by the flesh." (Galatians 3:3)

Jesus Grew

"And the child continued to grow and become strong in spirit, increasing in wisdom and the grace of God was on him." (Luke 2:40)

So starts the section on Jesus' childhood in Luke chapter 2, a section that finishes with,

"And Jesus kept increasing in wisdom, character[11] and favour with God and men" (Luke 2:52)

This verse covers a period of nearly twenty years in Jesus' life. For at least these twenty years and probably the twelve years before and the three and half to follow, Jesus grew in three dimensions.

- He grew in knowledge, understanding and **wisdom**.
- He grew in inner strength and **character**.
- He grew in **favour** with God and with others.

This is an amazing verse when you stop to think about it.

Maybe we can accept that Jesus had to learn some facts to grow in wisdom. But the idea of Jesus needing to grow in character is a bit harder. If Jesus had more character day by day, does that mean He had character deficiencies in the past? We will explore this further, but what should really surprise us is that Jesus grew in favour with God.

Jesus Grew in Favour

It is easy to understand how Jesus would grow in favour with other people. But how can it be that Jesus grew in favour with His Father God? The word "favour" is the Greek word *charis* more often translated as "grace". Surely this verse can't be saying that when

Jesus was a teenager God had more grace for Him than when He was a child? Surely His Father always loved Jesus and favoured Him the same?

Part of the solution to this problem is found in the reason why the translators of our Bibles sometimes translate "charis" as "grace" and sometimes translate it as "favour". The logic behind which way charis is translated seems to be based on whether it is being given or received. When it is given it is "grace", when it is received it is "favour".[12] So the "grace of God" that was on Jesus as a child in verse 40 has become the increasing "favour with God" of the young adult Jesus in verse 52.

The grace that the Father was pouring out on Jesus was not necessarily increasing, but Jesus' ability to capture that grace so that it stuck to Him was. As Jesus grew by experience in wisdom and character, so the grace of God poured out on Him and stuck to Him more and more as favour.

God has no favourites, but His favour sticks to some people much more than it does to others.

This is an important principle to get hold of. God pours His love and grace out on all mankind without prejudice. He pours out the same levels of grace on you as He poured out on Jesus. But **it is how that grace is received and how it sticks to us that determines how much favour our lives exhibit.** We do not earn God's favour, but there are principles for living that make us more sticky when it comes to grace.

Jesus Grew in Character

On the cross Jesus was to face the biggest injustice history has ever seen. Jesus, who was sinless, was going to carry the consequences of the entire world's sin and He was going to do it without bitterness or reproach. I used to think that the devil didn't realise what would happen if he took Jesus' life on the cross. Today I am inclined to think that he did know what would happen if he took the life of a sinless and submitted Jesus. However, the devil did not believe that *in his humanity* Jesus could suffer the injustice of experiencing all of mankind's God-forsakenness without feeling anger towards His Father, towards man or both (Luke 23:34). But it was in those moments between crying out, *"My God, my God, why have you forsaken me"* (Matthew 27:46) and then saying, *"Father, into your hand I commit this my Spirit"* (Luke 23:46) that the character of Jesus was truly tested.

I think that in those moments we must assume that Jesus' sense of the Spirit *on* Him and *with* Him were gone, and when the Spirit is not *on* us or *with* us it is also so much harder to discern the Spirit *in* us too (because the Spirit in us tends to leap up to connect with the Spirit on and around us). Jesus was left in His stripped back humanity with just faith in His Father's love and goodness to sustain an open heart towards God. And Jesus passed the test, because His character had been formed over the years to be ready for this test.

"Then the Lord said to Cain ... sin is crouching at your door, it desires you, but you must master it." (Genesis 4:6-7)

Like Cain, Jesus was born into an environment of sin, and like Cain, it was Jesus' responsibility to master the sin crouching at His door and not let it into His soul. As a child, Jesus would have encountered injustice, but a child's vision is limited and so the depth to which he/she feels injustice is limited and the situations they understand as being "unjust" are simple. So perhaps as a refugee in Egypt Jesus knew what it was like to be picked on for having a different accent. As He got older He would have understood the injustice of occupation by a harsh foreign power. As a child, Jesus only had to respond to these situations with the maturity of a child, but He did so without letting sin into His soul and every time He mastered sin, His character was growing. On the cross the whole slough of human sin came pressing in on Him, but

Jesus still didn't let it into His heart. So when the moment of death came and the devil still had nothing on Jesus, hell was left with an almighty problem! It had taken a life over which it had no claim.

There is a definite link between the victories we win in our hearts and the longer term authority we see active in our actions. Becoming like Jesus means that, like Him, we will rise above the bad heart attitudes and behaviours of the culture around us by absorbing sin's consequences without being infected by it or passing it on to someone else.

Jesus Grew in Wisdom

In the normal course of life, we will all grow in knowledge and understanding. Knowledge should lead to understanding and understanding can lead to wisdom, but it doesn't always. Wisdom doesn't arise simply by cramming your head full of more facts and insights. Wisdom is found in the creative *application* of what is known, so that it can release the full potential of the situation or person that surrounds it.

Jesus' wisdom was commented on by His critics (Mark 6:2), by Himself (Luke 11:31) and by His followers (John 1:1). What marked out Jesus' wisdom was that He took the same commonly acknowledged facts and saw totally different meaning and connections in them. When Scripture excluded lepers from the temple, everyone assumed that they were rejected by God, but Jesus understood the lesson that in the place of God's presence there was no sickness. So if Jesus was "Immanuel" - "God with us" - sicknesses should go when He arrived!

Wisdom only comes by taking the time to process life's lessons and experiences with the Lord (Father, Son and Holy Spirit). Jesus took time out at the ends and beginnings of days in order to pray (Mark 1:35; 6:46). By seeking heaven's perspective on events and situations, Jesus developed a wisdom in the application of truth that re-wrote the rulebook, but was also demonstrably superior to the wisdom others had in that it released life not death.

Jesus had to grow into the fullness that was for Him in God. He did so perfectly, but as a twelve-year old He exhibited the wisdom, character and favour appropriate to that life stage and development. In His twenties He did the same. In His thirties we saw His public "revealing" as a fit heir of the kingdom when, in a public ceremony, the Father publicly affirmed Him and gave Him access to the resources of heaven in a new way.

Jesus Lived From the Perspective of Heaven

Before Jesus started His public ministry, He came to be baptised by his cousin, John. As Jesus came up out of the water, *"the heavens were opened (to him)"*[13] (Matthew 3:16; Luke 3:22) and the Holy Spirit came on Him in a new way. Out of the open heavens there came the sound of rumbling thunder in which Jesus heard the Father speak the words, *"This is my beloved son, in whom I am well pleased."* Mark's gospel uses the phrase, *"the heavens were opening"* rather than *"were opened".* The Greek word is in the continuous tense to emphasise that the heavens were now continuously open to Jesus; they opened and they stayed open. This is a new experience for Jesus.

When the Spirit came on Jesus at His baptism it gave Him new access to the purposes, plans and perspectives of heaven. It also made Jesus more aware of the spiritual world around Him, so in the days following His "open heaven" experience He is rebuking the devil and then conversing with angels (Mark 1:13). For Jesus, life in the Spirit was, by its very nature, shaped and directed by fresh day-by-day words from heaven.

In the wilderness, the devil's first temptation is for Jesus to use His recently revealed status as the *"Son of God"* to feed Himself and turn rocks into bread rolls.

"If you are the Son of God, order these stones to become bread." (Matt 4:3; Luke 4:3)

But a fresh situation requires a fresh revelation. As "Son of Man", Jesus' role was not to live on self-aggrandising miracles nor the demands and wisdom of His flesh, because, as Jesus answers to the devil,

"Man shall not live by bread alone, but by every word that proceeds from the mouth of God." (Matthew 4:4).

Like the manna referenced by Jesus in His reply, the words Jesus was feeding on were fresh. They were the words proceeding from His Father each day, because you don't live on yesterday's manna, (Exodus 16:20). As the Son of God, Jesus had the power, but as the Son of Man He was looking for heaven's perspective on the rocks into rolls idea. Jesus lived by hearing heaven.

In a later book in this series we will look at the mechanisms of hearing heaven in a lot more detail. Jesus promised that His sheep would hear His voice and that we should be faithful in the use of what we have heard. So for this book I will assume that everyone reading this will know at some level how to hear God speak and that we will all improve in our hearing abilities the more deliberate practice we put in at listening. We can do this by making space for Jesus to speak to us and by being proactive in seeking Him for answers. This is how Jesus got hold of the words He needed.

"I have power to do nothing on my own initiative. As I hear, I decide and my decision is right because I don't seek my own purpose, but the purpose of Him who sent me."[14] (John 5:30)

Sometimes these words came down to Jesus, *"as I hear"*, and sometimes Jesus had to go up and find them: *"I ... seek ... the purpose of Him who sent me."* We hear from God in the same two ways. But either way, the purposes of heaven are effectively released onto earth through our constructive reaction to revelation.

The more I have learnt to live out of fresh revelation, the more I have found that I see Jesus being deliberate in getting hold of it in the gospels. I notice now how, in the accounts of Jesus' healings, Mark and Luke often describe a process. Jesus talks to the person, He takes them aside from the crowd, He does something different like making mud or telling them to go and do something. Or when an unusual situation arises Jesus draws in the dirt or initially deflects the request. I now recognise these actions as the side effects and outcomes of a dialogue with heaven about the person or situation at hand. Revelation often comes *"in part"* (1 Corinthians 13:9), but as we act on the part we have, more flows.

Life in the Spirit is sustained by fresh revelation while the religious life feeds on yesterday's news.

Life As Jesus Knew It

*"God sent out **His Son, born of a woman, born under the law**, so that He might redeem those who were under the law, so that we might receive our adoption as sons."* (Galatians 4:4-5)

This has been a very short consideration of the life lessons pioneered and modelled for us by Jesus. We have seen in brief how as Son of Man, Jesus lived a human life the way it was supposed to be lived.

- In constant awareness of the Spirit in, on and with Him.
- Growing in wisdom, character and favour.
- Listening for revelation to shape Him, lead Him and empower Him.

In these next chapters we will be exploring this way of living from the perspective of the follower. As followers we will need to learn from our failures as well as our successes, but we must not lose sight of the fact that Jesus is the standard we are called to. He is the horizon ahead of us.

Endnotes:

1. The only two places that the KJV ever translates the Greek word *"anothen"* as "again" are in this passage. In all other places it use "from above" or a similar concept of being higher.

2. "Born of water" (John 3:4) is a reference to the birth waters, not water baptism.

3. Only John's Gospel make a distinction between different modes of the Holy Spirit's operation in and to both Jesus and us as disciples. This is not surprising as John's Gospel is deliberate in revealing the spiritual and heavenly nature of Jesus.

4. Jesus implies to Nicodemus that earthly analogies are limited in their ability to explain the heavenly realms which need to be experienced directly (John 3:12).

5. For some unknown reason the NASB misses out the word *"pneuma"* which means "spirit" in its translation. Almost every other translation includes it.

6. In Greek *"pneuma"* is the penultimate word, "my" being the last and from John's Gospel we know that Jesus also spoke the words, "It is finished." But we don't know if He said that before or after commiting His spirit to the Father.

7. The definite article exists in the Greek texts but most versions ignore it. I have included it here as "this" because it highlights that Jesus is saying something specific about His spirit.

8. Mark and Luke use a weaker phrase which simply means "breath out" or "spirit leaves", so some translations will say something like, "He breathed his last". Matthew and John spell out the process of the spirit being yielded up more thoroughly.

9. The concept of an eternally unchanging God crept into Christianity from Greek philosophy and has been popular with theologians ever since. But an unchanging God is a dead God, because change is intrinsic to life. An unchanging God is not a Creator because He never has an original thought. But the God of the Bible has new mercies every day and His peace and government increase eternally.

10. It is a clear implication of New Testament teaching that now seated in the heart of the Trinity is a "man" who has been victorious in all situations and that this changes our relationship with God and His with us.

11. I have translated the word *"helikia"* as "character" rather than the more common "stature". The word is literally a measure of maturity in age or height, but as with the English word "stature" it is used metaphorically for the character of a person, and this is I believe its meaning in this verse, because to say Jesus grew in age is unnecessary and to say He grew in stature implies that His height was worth commenting on, whereas Isaiah prophesies that Jesus had no physical features that made Him stand out (Isaiah 53:2).

12. The same logic is used by translators in the Old Testament where the Hebrew word *"chen"* is also translated "grace" or "favour" dependent on whether it is being given or received.

13. Some early manuscripts of Matthew's account of this event add the words "to him" to emphasise that this was an experience for Jesus to walk in rather than as a sign to the general public.

14. Translation comment: the word normally translated "able to" or "can" is *"dunamia"*, related to the idea of power as in the English words "dynamic" or "dynamite". Similarly, the words normally translated "judge" and "judgement" are more naturally simply "decide" and "decision". "Purpose" is also a translation equivalent to the word normally translated "will".

3: Heirs of Promise

"... the anxious longing of creation waits eagerly for the ***revealing*** *of the sons of God ... in the hope that creation itself would also be set free from its slavery to decay into the freedom of the glory of God's children."*
(Romans 8:19-21)

In the ancient world the "revealing" of a son was a public event. It was the public recognition by a father that their nominated or adopted heir was mature enough to represent the household and to participate in their inheritance now. The form and significance of these ceremonies varied from region to region, but they were common across the Roman, Greek and Jewish world of Jesus' day.

At his baptism, Jesus' Heavenly Father responded to Him in a way that the ancient world would have understood as a "revealing" ceremony, a public recognition of Jesus as heir and "owner of everything" (Galatians 4:1).

We have already read that our destiny is to be just like Jesus *"the first born in a big family"* (Romans 8:29). Here we see that creation is desperately waiting for Jesus' co-heirs to step into the maturity and the promises of God that will free creation from its slavery to corruption. The world needs you to achieve your destiny and become who Jesus would be if He were you.

In between these verses (Romans 8:19-21) about liberating creation into the *"glory of God's children"* and the big family of people who are like Jesus (Romans 8:29), Paul writes about our need to cooperate with the Holy Spirit. He works for us and in us; He helps our weakness; He intervenes effectively for us and searches our hearts.

At some level we all cooperate with the Holy Spirit. We all said "yes" to Jesus at some point and gave Him permission to be our Lord. We are all on the programme. But the speed with which we make progress varies. In this life some will cross more borders than others on their way to the horizon.

I have particular reason to be grateful that some people do step into the kind of spiritual authority that creation cries out for in this life.

I grew up in a Christian home and in fact I am a pastor's kid. It is so easy to inherit a faith that is second hand. As a younger teenager, I knew there was something unreal about my faith. I flip-flopped between mild rebellions and responding to every gospel message I heard. But what really triggered me coming alive was when I almost died!

Who Will Free Me From This Body of Death?

When you are fifteen, three months feels like a lifetime, but when the doctors decide that it is your life expectancy it tends to leave you feeling short changed!

It was March 1982. I had been experiencing odd symptoms for over two months: aches, pains, shortness of breath, but I hadn't treated them seriously. At the start of the year England is wet and cold and infections tend to do the rounds. I had been to see a doctor a couple of times, but as an immortal fifteen-year old I wasn't concerned. But by April I was lying in a hospital bed very afraid and very angry with God.

Eventually the symptoms had become so severe that a proper investigation was required. What was revealed was very sobering indeed. I had tumours throughout my lymph system and the cancer had crossed over into my spinal fluid. I was diagnosed with an aggressive, non-Hodgkin's lymphoma from which I was not likely to recover. Fortunately for me, death (like life) doesn't always work out the way you expect it to.

By nature I was stoically optimistic, but alone at night there was a cry of fear and anger that went up to a God, who for the last year I had tried to serve to the best of my natural abilities. I had changed friends, broken habits and taken ridicule to follow Him and now in return this is what I got, cancer!

But as I allowed room for my monologue at God to become a dialogue with Him, peace came in alongside my anxiety and fear ebbed. I knew the love of Father, not just the fact of God. I was ready to die now, even though I didn't want to. I was experiencing the truth of the verse that says,

*"... you haven't received a spirit of slavery, a return to fear. But you have received the Spirit of **adoption as sons** by which we cry "Daddy! Father!"* (Romans 8:15)

At the time I may not have put it quite like this, but my fear had opened me up to a dialogue that led me into the Father's arms in a way my shopping list prayers and whining apologies for failing Him never could. The Spirit in me brought me into an experience of sonship even in the midst of my confusion. That experience is called "adoption" in most translations of the Bible. In Greek the word is literally "son placement". The Holy Spirit that God placed in me was the Spirit that was in Jesus, the eternal Son. When you received the Holy Spirit, Jesus' experience of sonship was placed in you whether you are male or female.

In the ancient world adoption was more about placing a child in line for an inheritance than it was about changing families. So this verse implies more than just freedom from fear and a sense of God's fatherhood. It implies an inheritance, a promise to cross over into. It anticipates the "revealing" of mature heirs who free creation from its *"slavery to corruption and decay"* (Romans 8:19).

Cancer is such a clear example of this "corruption and decay". Living cells divide to make new cells, but damage occurs in such a way that damaged cells make more damaged cells. Useless cells multiply unchecked choking resources to healthy tissue.

I am so grateful to my heavenly Father that He is still nurturing and revealing sons and daughters who face the needs of this broken world and know how to access the riches of our heavenly inheritance to meet them; whose cooperation with the Holy Spirit creates great testimonies out of all sorts of situations.

So one night in April 1982, a Canadian man called Don Northrop came to visit me in hospital. He and the leaders of my church laid hands on me and rebuked the cancer in the name of Jesus. My consultant was not at all happy about this. He had told my parents it would be better if they could accept what was happening to me rather than "clutching at straws". The next day after being prayed for, when the same doctor came to examine me, he joked, "Okay, let's exorcise this demon!" A few minutes later he muttered to himself, "Oh, that's odd."

"What is?" I asked.

"Oh, it's just that I can't feel the swelling under your arm. Still these things are unpredictable - it may have softened a bit."

From that day forward, no cancer was found in my body ever again. I had had an encounter with God, yes, but also in Don, with one of His revealed sons - someone my broken creation was crying out for. And it changed me.

You will also appreciate why I'm glad Don did not treat his inheritance as an optional extra and why I don't want to treat mine (nor you to treat yours), lightly either. But so few Christians really reflect the maturity of Jesus. While most of the world believes in God, they are not too impressed by His ground crew.

Today I can say that I live the supra-natural life more than I did ten years ago, but my own journey towards the promised horizon has not been without its delays and frustrations.

Sometimes it's easier to know what you've been saved from than it is to know what you've been saved for!

Out of Egypt

"So family, I do not want you to be ignorant. All our fathers were under the cloud, and all passed through the sea. And all were baptised to Moses in the cloud and in the sea, and all ate the same spiritual food and drank the same spiritual drink (they drank from the spiritual Rock that followed them, and that Rock was Christ). **But with many of them God was not very happy, because they were undone by the wilderness.** *Now these are an example for us."* (1 Corinthians 10:1-6a)

In Israel's formation as a nation there were two great "baptism" events: the crossing of the Red Sea, which took them from **slavery into freedom**, and the crossing of the Jordan, which took them **from freedom into promise**.

Between the Red Sea and the Jordan was the wilderness. The journey through the wilderness should have been a two and a half year season of transformation, a preparation period of incredible blessing and favour that was supposed to fit Israel for possessing the Promised Land. Instead, according to this passage above, the wilderness proved to be their undoing. Thirty months of preparation became a lifetime of aimless wandering, albeit one that was blessed by the presence and provision of a loving God.

For two and a half years after leaving Egypt everything went so well for the Israelites. Despite their complaints, God cleansed bitter water for them to drink and released more water from a rock. He supernaturally supplied manna and quails to eat. He forgave the people's idolatry, put His presence in their midst and protected them in battle. God established His relationship with the Israelites through the Law, the ark, the priests and the tabernacle. But when the opportunity and challenge came to cross the Jordan and step into their inheritance, God's people were not ready.

They balked at their first opportunity for a baptism that would take them from freedom into promise. The pattern the Israelites modelled seems so often to be the pattern our own lives.

We make it to freedom, but don't step into promise.

There are oases in the desert, but they are not the promised land. A season of favour is not a sign of arrival, it is preparation for the life of promise.

Seasons of Favour

I met Paul in a bar on the sea front in Lowestoft, Britain's most easterly town. It was the mid 80s and the first evening of our outreach was a drizzly summer night. He was friendly and came back with us to the double-decker bus that doubled as a coffee bar and a centre for our evangelism. I told him things I had seen Jesus do in people's lives and some healing stories. At the end of the evening he asked me how to become a Christian. He received Jesus and immediately felt different. A great start to our week, there would be plenty of time to help Paul discover more of Jesus.

But then Paul told me that he started a residential work-skills course the next day on account of his disability. It turned out he had clubfoot.[1] He asked if we could pray for his foot and we agreed of course. We prayed and that night he *ran* back to his parent's home completely healed.

The next morning Paul rang the training centre to tell them he wasn't coming as he was no longer disabled. The centre told him that if he didn't turn up they would charge the cost of the course directly to him. If he did turn up, then the local authority picked up the bill. So Paul went to attend the course, but bought a Bible on the way.

On the course was a man who said he was a Christian, but he was also a spiritualist. He offered to teach Paul some things about his new faith. That night Paul opened his new Bible at random and the first words he read were in Leviticus: *"Don't consult with mediums..."* (Leviticus 19:31). Paul showed the verse to his classmate and was saved from some unhelpful conversations.

Seaside towns are full of spiritualism and back on the sea front I met another medium called Chris. As we talked I became aware of demonic spirits starting to gather around us. I could "see" them in my spirit. Chris was surprised that I knew what was happening as in his experience most Christians seemed unaware of the realms he operated in. In the end, Chris wasn't ready to change his life. He had several affairs going on with the wives and girlfriends of the trawler men that operate out of Lowestoft.

During those days, I had my first word of knowledge for someone outside of a church meeting context.

Over the week around twenty adults and many children made choices to follow Jesus. We were pleased and had been inviting everyone we met to a final barbeque. On the afternoon of the barbeque it started to rain, heavily. As the team tried to light the grills under plastic sheets, Danny (who was leading the outreach and drove the double-decker) and I walked around the green where we had parked our bus. We prayed for sun and rebuked the clouds. We were thrilled when the rain stopped and sunshine lit up the area around our base. Amazingly, the green was the only spot on the sea front where it wasn't raining! People started gathering on it from all directions to avoid the rain elsewhere, just as we started our barbeque and testimonies.

The next day, we baptised a number of young men, including Paul, at a local Baptist church. Paul still wanted to find out more about his new faith. I was due to leave for home in London, but as I was Paul's first contact I felt a responsibility for him.

That night I read James 4, where it says, *"Come on, you who say tomorrow I will go to such and such a city ... When in fact you don't know what tomorrow will hold."* (James 4:13-24). I didn't think much of this until the next day. As I drove back to London from Lowestoft, wondering how Paul would settle into a local church, my car engine blew up. I was just outside Thetford, sixty miles from Lowestoft and eighty miles from home in London. I realised I was about to find out what the verses I had read the night before were all about.

I sat on the roadside wondering what to do when Mark, the brother of Danny who led the outreach, drove past and recognised me. Mark lived in Thetford. He had met me only briefly the weekend before when he had come up to Lowestoft to see how the outreach was going. He towed my car back to his house while I wondered what to do with a dead car.

Mark's neighbour was a mechanic. He checked over the car and confirmed that the cylinder rings had blown and I would need a new engine. Amazingly, the neighbour had just removed a good working engine from a wrecked car that would fit mine perfectly. He owed Mark some favours so offered to put the engine into my car at cost, £70, but he would do it in his spare time, so it would take ten to fourteen days. Despite this incredible provision (a replacement engine would normally have cost several hundred pounds, even in the 1980s), I didn't have the money as I was a poor nineteen-year old student.

I knew I should go back to Lowestoft and see Paul, so I prayed that I would find some short-term work to pay for the repairs. I made some calls and went back to stay with a couple, John and Maria, who had sponsored the outreach and who lived about a mile from Paul's parents. The next day they mentioned my predicament to a man in their church. He managed a local shoe factory and the factory needed a kitchen hand in their canteen to provide two weeks cover, so I started frying chips and making sandwiches the next day!

Over the next two weeks, I got to spend each evening with Paul, introducing him to other Christians, taking him to church and answering his questions. I met his sister and her husband, who both made a commitment to Jesus too. At the end of the fortnight, I had earned exactly enough money to give a gift to my hosts and pay for my car repairs.

On the night I went back to Mark's house to collect my car, a friend of his came over. I told him my testimony and we all talked. In the early hours of the morning he gave his life to Jesus.

I've been brief in my description of August 1985. There are lots of things I could have added. Paul's introduction to Christianity was full of supra-natural excitement, healings, divine direction and guidance, unusual patterning of events, financial provisions and more. In the wider context there were demonic encounters, revelations and miracles and I knew the favour of God on me.

I stayed in touch with Paul for a couple of years. Sadly, during this time his experience of church changed his expectations. Following Jesus lost its adventure. His faith became about a free ticket to heaven when you die. There were some things to learn along the way and some behaviour management techniques to adopt. Paul went less and less to church until he had effectively dropped out, then we lost touch.

My own life didn't move seamlessly from glory to glory either. Life became more routine, my relationship with Jesus more a habit. Before I knew it, I was seeing far less of the supra-natural life than I had before. But I told myself there were "seasons of favour" and that was that! It was down to God to do something new if He wanted to and I had a stack of good stories to share when I needed to impress someone. Everyone seems to walk in a season of favour when they first get saved. The details might be very different dependent on the expectations and theology of the context you got saved in, but we all know God is good, that Jesus loves us and that we are going to rock the world for Him.

With the passing of time, however, many of us can also identify with David's prayer to *"restore to me the joy of my salvation"* (Psalm 51:12). At some point the manna gets boring. Eventually, I settled for the same old manna day in, day out.[2]

My observation at the time was that I was not alone. It seemed that others were also, like me, stuck in a predictable Christian limbo.

All too often Jesus becomes like a rock band we've followed for years. His greatest hits seem to be in His back catalogue and just maybe every now and again He provides a taste of something that excites us like it did in our spiritual youth.

When this happens it is almost certain that we have missed an opportunity to cross a border into a new season of life, into more of His promise to us. Sometimes we are aware of the missed opportunity and other times the Lord lets it pass us by unnoticed, knowing that we are not yet ready for the challenges the new territory represents.

It doesn't have to be like this! We were made for more!

Why settle for a good but repetitive life when we can grow from glory to glory?

The Relatively Successful Christian Life!

So as life went on I settled into a routine. I still saw answers to prayer, I still had successes, but success is not quite the same as fruit. Success is something you aim for and achieve, something that is out of your ordinary. Fruit, on the other hand, is something that grows naturally because a tree is healthy. There are other differences as well, between "success" and "fruitfulness", but for now I just want to say that once we start confusing the two it is not long before the devil has us chasing our tails, trying to re-capture a lost season by achieving its successes all over again. Then when that doesn't work we get disappointed or tired and we lower our levels of hope and expectation. When our hope has diminished, then by definition our faith has got smaller, because faith is the assurance of the things we hope for (Hebrews 11:1). Smaller hopes, smaller faith.

At this time of my life, I didn't really notice it, but as I look back now I realise that I was seeing less in terms of healings, less salvations and less divine connections and coincidences. In other areas I still knew real blessing. In particular I knew Father's favour on the *"work of my hand"* (Deuteronomy 2:7). I started a ministry that gave me national recognition. I met Archbishops and the heads of all the major denominations in England. I instigated a prayer event that drew 11,000 people. In 1995 I led the UK delegation to the Global Congress on World Evangelisation in Korea. Father was still blessing me, but life was now more about what I was doing for God, rather than what God's life was doing in and through me. Life was successful in a natural way, rather than supra-naturally fruitful.

I was settling for less than I could have been, not because I was lazy in spiritual things, but because there were lessons I hadn't learnt, coupled with misguided expectations resulting in passivity when I should have been active and striving in the things I should have simply received by faith. Crucially, there was also pride in what I had already seen and achieved. Put simply, I found security in my testimony when it should have been my inspiration.

Back on Track

Today, I'm glad I can say that I live the supra-natural life more than I did ten years ago. I've learned how to stay fresh in the Spirit and I more regularly see the miraculous and I hear Jesus more clearly. I feel the Spirit in me, loving me, encouraging me and changing me. I find creative wisdom that benefits those around me with surprising solutions. Seemingly trivial connections and events come back years later with increased significance and possibility.

Life is supra-natural, but in the most natural way - so natural that the miraculous seems normal until I write things down in my journal and reflect on how amazing events are.

To illustrate, today a lady's leg was healed as I preached. She had not been able to straighten it and had had pain for months. Yesterday, I prayed for an injury from a horse kick that had lasted for months and today there is no lump or pain. Neither of these felt special or magical. In the first case mentioned, I knew nothing about it until after the meeting when the lady in question showed me how her very normal leg could straighten out in a very normal way, just like everyone else's. It is often only on reflection I realise that while I prayed or while I spoke, the purposes of heaven were being done on earth.

At one level, it would be true to say that I don't know why these things happen to some people and not to others, but actually I would not be being entirely honest. I do know what has made the difference in me and I have tried to pass my lessons on to people in River Church and others have found the lessons work for them too. This book is my attempt to start to pass on to the wider body of Jesus those same lessons. I want to pull out some foundational assumptions, but before we do let's go back to the Jordan where the Israelites stand at the crossroads of destiny.

Will they be heirs of promise?

Plundering or Possessing Promise

As stated previously, it need only have technically taken a month to reach the Promised Land. In reality, however, despite their spectacular and miraculous salvation testimony, God knew that the Israelites would need an on-going and varied experience of His love and provision before they would be ready to cross the Jordan and possess their inheritance.

"A hastily gained inheritance is not a blessing in the end" (Proverbs 20:21)

So instead of leading them on a thirty-day stampede northward and straight into Canaan, God led them south and east into the wilderness of the Sinai peninsular and into a period of provision and favour. Then after two and a half years, God led the Israelites to the edge of the Jordan where they caught sight of their inheritance.

Twelve men were sent into Canaan to see what it was like. They came back carrying stolen fruit, but they also brought back reports of the strength of the incumbent people. Of the twelve spies, only two of them believed they could possess their inheritance. You know the story, I'm sure.

The reaction of the people was to complain. God asks them to do something impossible, to take a risk for which they are not ready. The people lose sight of the power of the testimony they have already and so they don't step into the testimony that could have been theirs. God sums it up like this:

*"All those who have **seen my glory, and my signs**, done in Egypt and in the wilderness, but have still tested me ten times, **and haven't listened** to me; they shall not see the land which I promised to their fathers, nor shall any of those who **did not honour me** see it: but my servant Caleb, **because he had a different spirit in him** and has followed me fully, I will bring him into the land he went into; and his descendants shall possess it."* (Numbers 14:22-24)

Two million adults had come out of slavery in Egypt, but now only two were ready to complete the journey into the Promised Land.[3] The rest would never be ready.

It would have been unreasonable if God had expected the Israelites to change overnight, so He didn't. The combination of His tangible presence ("my glory") with them and the things He did for them ("my signs") should have been enough to change them for good! Thirty days would have been too quick, but thirty months should have been sufficient. But "ten times" the Israelites failed to "listen" with faith and they had not honoured God for what He was doing, but rather complained about what He wasn't doing.

Can it really be only one in a million that makes it?[4] Fortunately, this history is recorded for our instruction, it is not prescriptive in our situation. We can do better! You can step into your inheritance in this life.

I think the key is the need to "listen" if we are going to be changed. To listen to someone is probably the simplest way in which we can honour them. There is a really important principle here. Every time God did something for the Israelites He was speaking to them. His interventions were the *"word of His grace which has power to build you up and give you an inheritance"* (Acts 20:32). When the people failed to follow God's presence into the Promised Land, they had already failed on nine previous occasions to be changed by God's words of grace to them.

A friend, Nigel, once commented that he had spent a fair amount of time in life being driven to places by people and there were some drivers with whom *every journey was an experience* and there were others who were *experienced drivers*. The two are not the same thing.

The things God does to us and through us are supposed to renew us!

A succession of experiences doesn't necessarily make you experienced. Experiences have to be internalised in the right way, so that the lessons learned continue with you and in you; they build together, *"line on line, line on line, precept upon precept, precept upon precept, a little here a little there."* (Isaiah 28:10).

Actually there is also an important flip side to this. There is a level of authority in any field that cannot be achieved without experience. There is an authority that has to be *grown into*. The Israelites needed the thirty months of blessing. They *needed* to practice the response of faith several times before they would be ready to cross the Jordan.

Similarly, Jesus lived thirty years before He presented Himself at the Jordan to pass through it in baptism and into the ministry and life He had been born for. When the Father spoke from heaven and affirmed His pleasure in His son (Luke 3:22) it was because Jesus had been successfully shaped and formed over the course of His life up to that point. He had grown *"in wisdom, character and favour"* (Luke 2:52) and was now ready to step into His calling.

And so it is with us. Every experience of God's grace has the potential to teach us and change us if we will listen. But most of us have not been taught how to process our history and testimony.

Now here is a sobering thought. Even though the children of Israel had failed nine times already, God still presented them with the opportunity to succeed on the big occasion. Just because rehearsals had gone badly, God didn't cancel the opening night. This happens in our lives all the time. I have to confess it has happened to me often. Father has opened doors for me that I was not ready to go through and I realise now that it was because I had failed to learn the things He had been teaching me along the way.

The point of letting the twelve spies go into the Promised Land and to plunder its produce was to inspire everyone with the benefits of living there. Of those adults who stood on the edge of promise just thirty months after their salvation, only Caleb and Joshua were going to achieve what they had been set free for. This was because there was something different about their inner lives; Caleb *"had a different spirit in him"*.

You can set someone free, but you can't free someone who's set. Everything God did for the Israelites in the wilderness had a lesson in it that could have changed the people, but most treated these interventions of grace as a show to be enjoyed today and forgotten tomorrow.

- *When God turned the bitter waters sweet* (Exodus 15:25): Caleb understood that "God was the healer" of their bitter spirits (Exodus 15:26). Most worried about what they would eat next (Exodus 16:3).

- *When God gave them manna that tasted like honey* (Exodus 16:31): Caleb tasted the promise of a new land flowing with milk and honey (Numbers 13:27,30). Most compared it unfavourably with the food they had back in Egypt (Numbers 11:4-6).

- *When God protected the Israelites from the attack of the Amalekites* (Exodus 17:8): Caleb understood "God was their banner" (Exodus 17:15). Most thought they had just got lucky (Numbers 13:28-33).

Caleb's spirit cooperated with the blessing and grace it experienced day by day. He soaked it up like water on a sponge and it gave him weight and authority. His contemporaries, on the other hand, proved to be as impervious as ducks backs to the showers of blessing they experienced. It was the failure in the little opportunities along the way that meant that when God opened a door to their destiny, most people were not ready to go and slay some giants and live in promise. It is the way we respond to what God does to us and through us that makes all the difference.

When the grace that God pours onto us gets into us, it becomes favour and favour is a hallmark of the supra-natural life.

Whoever you are, you live under grace. So what God does for you and through you is, by definition, *beyond* what you deserve. The point of the supra-natural life is not to collect stories of "favour" to be worn like scout badges on our church uniform: "Yes, I have the 'Healed a Bad Back' badge. I notice you have the 'Medium Sized Financial Provision' badge. Tell me about it!"

The point of the supra-natural life is to let the truth that is being revealed by grace to us, into our hearts where it changes us and becomes favour and results in the evidence of a life shaped by grace. The supra-natural life is a life lived by cooperation with the Holy Spirit. Growth doesn't come either by trying harder or by waiting passively. It comes by acknowledging, listening and responding to God.

"As a man(he) thinks in his heart, so he is." (Proverbs 23:7)

If our hearts are full of what God has done for us, then who we are will be who He is shaping us to be. If our hearts are full of what He has not done for us yet, then who we are will shaped by disappointment in a vacuum! Learning to focus on and cooperate with what God is doing in and around us is a simple discipline that makes a radical difference to the nature of our Christian life.

The truth is, any idiot can plunder the Promised Land, but Father is looking for people fit to farm it and make it fruitful with Him.

Perhaps it is a bit unkind to use the term "any idiot", but I wanted to make the point forcefully. The point of letting the spies go into the land, to experience it and experience its fruit, was to inspire all the people with the idea of living there. In seasons of favour, God is trying to get us addicted to the supra-natural life, but He is also showing us what it will take to sustain life beyond the Jordan.

Whoever you are and whatever your maturity is in Jesus you always have the possibility of plundering your promises rather than possessing them.

I guess the Israelites could have made the stealing of fruit an annual event. Every year send in small guerrilla forces that avoided being seen, steal some fruit and come home. But every year it would have been the same old miracle, there would be no thrill of seeing beyond what they could ask for or think. They would never have progressed to see the ornamental grapes, figs and pomegranates that would, in the future, adorn Solomon's Temple - a wonder of the ancient world, the dwelling place of the presence of God.

Life would be lived out of programme not presence!

The entire resources of heaven are potentially available for us to plunder our promises at any time. God's grace makes all things possible to you through faith, whatever your maturity or moral condition. But Father is looking for His children to grow to maturity, because we were made for partnership with Him. He looks for us to grow into the grace He has given us so we can receive even more. He wants you to be the rightful possessor of your promises.

While Jesus gives the Spirit without measure, in practice His grace sets the limits on how much favour and authority actually sticks to us - limits that reflect, but are not constrained by, our maturity. God always gives us more than we deserve. In fact, He also gives us far more than is safe for us and others around. When it comes to spiritual authority **Jesus gives us enough rope to hang ourselves, but not so much that this is an inevitability!**

As we mature in what we have been given, He entrusts us with more. This is not earning our salvation, but it is the *"working out of our salvation"* that we are told to do (Philippians 2:12). We live in the truth of *"whoever is faithful in the very little is also faithful in much"* (Luke 16:10).

What Have We Learnt?

The foundation of all spiritual transformation is the grace, initiative and love of God. While He initiates He expects us to cooperate.

You may have noticed as you read this book, that I am very aware of my own journey with Jesus. Actually, I have found that there has been a connection between my deepening experience of God and my recognition of my story in Him. Taking time to listen with faith to your own testimony honours Jesus and is a very powerful thing. So before proceeding...

1. Think about your own salvation and the story that led up to it: When did it happen? What was the route to it? Was it a crisis

moment or a gradual process? Who were the important individuals along the way?

2. Now make a list of the key people, events and decision points on the journey with space to add more information.

3. Ask Jesus to show you more. Are there details you have forgotten? Are there things Jesus wants to say to you through your story? Do you feel or see any connections between the events of your story and particular Biblical characters?

4. Make a note of what Jesus shows you.

5. Now think about some of the highlights of your Christian life since you got saved. Choose one of these favoured moments and repeat steps 1 to 4.

6. Now thank Jesus for what he has done and ask him to start speaking to you through it.

Endnotes:

1. A condition from birth where the foot turns under severely, effectively causing the sufferer to walk on their ankle.

2. It might be surprising that I am using the provision of manna in a negative sense, after all Jesus uses it as both a metaphor for Himself, "I am the bread of life" and it is behind "give us today our daily bread". But in Deuteronomy 8, God highlights that the Israelites had settled for the provision of manna (v3, v16) rather than pressing into the Promised Land where the real blessing was (v7-10).

3. Joshua and Caleb.

4. The early Church experienced a much better ratio of "overcomers" to believers than 1 in a million. But since the beginning of the 20th Century the ratio of miracle-experiencing Christians to "safe believers" has boomed and the ratio continues to shift in favour of those who experience more of the "beyond what they ask or imagine".

4: Words of Grace

"Now I commend you to God and the word of His grace, which has power to build you up and give you an inheritance among all those who are sanctified." (Acts 20:32)

Paul spoke these words just as he was about to leave the leaders of the Ephesian church for what he knew would be the last time. It was a church that he had planted and deeply loved. Like so much of Paul's teaching, this verse deals with a process of transformation. It is a process that starts with a word of grace from God - a word that builds us up by our interaction with it, releasing us into an inheritance that is shared in common with all those who are mature in their sanctification.[1]

In one of his most famous parables, Jesus also told us about the effect of God's words of grace going out. In the parable of the "sower and the seed", some seeds (words from God) were eaten, some were burnt and some strangled, but some produced fruit. So when the word (seed) of God hits us, it might or it might not produce fruit.

The same ambiguity exists in the verse above. Words of grace have the effective ability, "the power", to grow us and take us into the inheritance of those who are "sanctified". But this is far from being an inevitable outcome in this life.

Back on Course

I have mentioned previously that my journey into the supra-natural life went through an uncertain phase. In the early nineties I was outwardly very successful in terms of ministry. I mixed with international church leaders and Christian ministries, I spoke at conferences, I sat on steering committees and boards for various missions and projects. In terms of profile I was far more successful than I am today. Recently, somebody asked me why I had "quit the Premier League to play in the Vauxhall conference division"? The only answer that makes sense of course is, "Well, this is how God led me!" which is absolutely true. But as I look back now, even I can see the grace and sense in what He did.

My Christian life had become professional and it was all about what I did for Jesus. I still seemed to be living in favour at one level, but at another I felt I was getting what I worked for, which made me proud and not very gracious. I was also getting very frustrated. It seemed like I had become the victim of my own success. I was living by my diary, not faith.

But then in the mid-nineties, Jesus called my wife Judith and me and our first two children out of London and, as it transpired, out of ministry. I hadn't realised just how much of my spiritual life was actually lived out of my function. Now I didn't have to preach I didn't know what to read in my Bible! I discovered prayer was not a life foundation for me, but an optional extra. Of course, this didn't stop me sometimes giving my "helpful" critiques to those leading the church we joined (there is a whole class of difficult people in churches today who are actually called as leaders, but who have dropped out of their calling for one reason or another).

After a few years of spiritual funk, the inner frustration that comes with being in the "wrong place" drew me back into a serious dialogue with Father. I knew I should be in ministry, but I was telling Him all the things I had not been happy with the first time around. In particular, I was frustrated with the lack of spiritual authority and power I had experienced at the end of my previous season in ministry.

It's not my desire to put disturbing images into your mind, but it is a matter of historical fact that I was redeeming time on the toilet one day by praying, talking to the Lord about precisely this lack of power. I told Jesus that I wasn't going to go back into ministry without more spiritual authority. As I made my case, a phrase came back into my head as clear as if it had been audible:

"The trouble is, Chris, you won't receive from those who have more breakthrough in this than you, because you compare their weaknesses against your strength."

It hit me like a slap in the face, but it wasn't a criticism, it was a word of grace! I knew instantly what Jesus meant.

My Dad is an exceptional man, once described in a history of the new denominations in the UK as "the finest mind in British Evangelicalism".[2] In addition he was also an activist church planter. I had the privilege of growing up and absorbing some of the best and freshest Bible teaching you are ever likely to find and, as a result, I had an instinct for the Bible and theology that has always given me an edge compared to my peers. But this incredible gift that was unearned and hardly worked for on my part became a pride and had made me highly selective of who and what I would receive from.[3]

When the word of God goes out, it has the potential to bear fruit. That challenge, spoken into my heart (while hitting me on the head!) was to lead me into a new way of living with Jesus. Many of my old securities and techniques in ministry had to be dismantled and re-built. There was a challenge to my earthly heritage, good though it was. There was a challenge to my pride and my identity, which was in what I had been and what I had done for Jesus, not in Jesus Himself. There was a challenge to me to honour and value faith over and above understanding, and to be humble in receiving from those who lived this instinctively, even if they couldn't justify the why or how of what they said and did with theological clarity or depth.

Looking back, I credit that undignified moment as the start of the next phase of my walk with Jesus. It led me back into ministry, but with a new humility and dependence, a new emphasis on presence over presentation. My natural heritage would have to be counted as loss for the privilege of knowing Jesus. I discovered a new sensitivity to Jesus' voice and I rediscovered what it was to live out of relationship with Him, rather than out of my natural skills, competencies and best laid plans. I had stepped back into the supra-natural life.

Words of Truth, Words of Love, Words of Favour

When Jesus got baptised, heaven spoke a word of grace over Him.

"This is my son, beloved, in whom I am very pleased." (Matthew 3:17)

This word of grace from heaven over Jesus was made up of three parts. It contained:

- *A word of Truth:* about who Jesus was, *"This is my son..."*
- *A word of Love:* about what the Father felt for Him, *"beloved".*
- *A word of Favour:* about how the Father felt about what He did, *"...in whom I am very pleased."*

Jesus needed the word of grace over Him in order to cross the Jordan and become the Messiah His Father needed Him to be. As the Son of Man, Jesus was living life the way we should be living it. So it's important to note that Jesus' response to the word of grace was to get away from the crowds and go to the wilderness to take time in the word He had just heard and to contend for it. A lifetime later one of Jesus' followers will write to a younger convert, telling him to use the words he has received by prophecy to fight the good fight (1 Timothy 1:18). It is because God's words of grace over us are powerful that they will be contested - though the battle is seldom about whether you will do a particular thing or not. Rather, the battle is about whether the word is going to become rooted in your soul or not. If it does, it is the nature of seed to grow and produce fruit, whether you understand how or not (Mark 4:27-28).

You may not feel that God has spoken over you, but this is a lie, He has. It is simply that His words of grace, like the seed in the parable, have been stolen, strangled or scorched out of us by the enemy. Learning to nurture the words heaven speaks over us is what gives the soil in our lives the depth to release their fruit.

Jesus says, *"My sheep hear my voice"* (John 10:27). It is a promise for all who follow Him. In the third book in this series we will look in detail at the different ways we are able to hear heaven, but theory is nowhere near as effective as practice at developing "ears to hear". If you will give time to deliberately listening and testing what you think you have heard by acting as if it is true, you will start to hear Jesus more clearly, more often and in a wider vocabulary.

Soul Food

I have divided up the words spoken to Jesus at His baptism into a "word of truth", a "word of love" and a "word of favour", and you have no doubt spotted the connection between the *wisdom, character* and *favour* that Jesus grew in. The reason this pattern emerges and the reason why God speaks words that can be categorised as Truth, Love and Favour into our hearts is not arbitrary. There is a battle going on over the human soul and these words of grace are precisely targeted missions from heaven to undo the damage in the soul caused by the devil, the father of lies, a murderer from the beginning and a thief (John 8:44, Mark 4:15).

The soul is the place where our spiritual and physical lives combine, where earth and heaven meet in us. It is the place where our decision making lies; it incorporates our emotions and ways of thinking.

The human soul receives input from both your body (the flesh) and your spirit.[4] From our bodies, input comes through our senses and memories (both conscious and subconscious). From our spirit, input comes from the heavens or spiritual realms, perhaps from the Holy Spirit, but maybe a demonic force or an angel. From these inputs our soul makes choices and sets a course of action for our lives. Neither the human soul, nor the flesh (our bodies) is intrinsically evil, it is simply the way in which we prioritise and use each that determines whether our actions release heaven's agenda, our agenda, the world's agenda, or Satan's agenda.

The cells in the physical body are constantly being replaced. In seven years time your body will not contain a single living cell that is in it today. But you will still be you. That is because it is your soul, not your body, that carries your story. And your story is unique! Our bodies get recycled and shared around (statistically you probably have two oxygen atoms from Julius Caesar's dying breath in your body right now). In the new heaven and earth we get a brand new body. So you are not your body, what makes you "you" is your story.

As our personal history unfolds, our souls carry forward the story we have lived so far, with all its consequences, failures and triumphs, the laughter and tears, the truth we have learned and the lies we have believed. It carries them into the life we are yet to live, shaping future decisions and reactions. Sadness and joy in the past will colour how we see and experience the world today. Your soul carries your unique story,[5] it is your soul that Jesus came to save and redeem.

So understanding how our souls have been damaged will help us understand how Jesus first fixes us, then redeems us. And why words of grace are not an option, they are the essence of human life. We live on the words that proceed from the mouth of God.

Lies, Fear and Famine

When mankind fell it was because Adam and Eve believed a spiritual lie. The lie was a subtle one: it questioned God's truthfulness: "you won't die". It questioned whether God really had man's best interests at heart: "God knows if you eat it you'll be like him in your knowledge of good and evil". And it questioned God's blessing by focusing on what man didn't have: "the tree in the middle" rather than everything he had been given: "any tree in the garden". So it questioned God's Truth, it questioned Gods' Love and it questioned God's Favour.

The Lie challenged Adam and Eve to consider the input of the flesh against the input of heaven. And according to Eve's fleshly senses, *"she **saw** that the tree was **good for food, a delight to the eyes** and **desirable.**"* (Genesis 3:6).

The Lie led mankind to trust their senses above God's word of grace. Testing the devil's claims by eating the fruit seemed to prove him right too. Because within the limits of their understanding, Adam and Eve didn't die and they had become the arbiters of what was good and what was evil without heavens help. From the perspective of their flesh the devils lie looked like truth.

In believing the Lie about who God was, mankind had also accepted a lie about who they were. They now believed that their identity, being god-like, was something to be attained by the things they did and that their flesh was capable of achieving spiritual goals without heaven's help.

"In the day you eat it your eyes will be opened and you will be like God." (Genesis 3:5)

In reality, the opposite was true. They were already made in God's image and had become human only because God had breathed His breath into them. Even mankind's fleshly existence was dependent on this residue of heaven left in them.

By eating the fruit, a new experience entered the soul of man. Not one shaped by the Truth of heaven, but by the Lie of hell. In man's soul, this new experience would re-shape his perception.

The Lie Became Our Reality

So in believing, testing and seemingly proving the Lie to be "true", mankind now has "evidence" not to trust heaven. The Lie about who God is, what man is and how we should live is now firmly rooted in man's soul, to be carried forward to inform his future as well as his present.

But mankind's fall didn't end with the Lie. When God comes looking for Adam, Adam hides, because he "was afraid". Instead of knowing love in God's presence he feels fear - not because God has stopped loving him, but because experience reflects our perception.

"When your eye is good, your whole body is also full of light; but when it is corrupt, your body also is full of darkness." (Luke 11:34).

I have a friend, Mara, who has a doctorate in Psychology. She tells me that our inner experience of reality is mostly perception. Our expectations, beliefs and emotional state trump cold hard facts every time. Adam's fear of God was real in him, even though there was no foundation for it in objective reality.

The fear he felt caused Adam to cover himself from others and to cover himself from God. Fear has started to shape man's soul even when he is not actually sinning. He is experiencing what should be a good life, but with a sin-sick soul, so life feels bad.

Fear in the heart tries to protect the real person with layer upon layer of persona. Perhaps it is this wilful covering, born out of fear, that has disrupted the ability of the human spirit to hear heaven clearly. Wrapping a fat hand around some mobile phones stops them receiving a signal. Fear in mankind's soul has killed our relationship with God and separated us from our source of life.

On the sixth day of creation, God had declared our flesh to be good, because it was in a role that served the spirit and the spirit heard heaven. It was through our flesh that the Father expected us to fulfil His commission to be *"fruitful, to multiply, to fill up and rule over the earth"* (Genesis 1:28). But man no longer trusts heaven and doesn't hear from it clearly either. So it is not a surprise that the fruitfulness and authority man used to have is lost.

Famine, futility and fruitlessness now become part of human experience, replacing the fruit and authority God had originally declared over him.

"...with hard work you shall bear children ... the ground is cursed because of you, with hard work you shall eat from it." (Genesis 3:16-17)

The Lie undermined God in the human heart, denying His Truth, Love and Favour. It skewed our understanding of who we are. Now, to be in God's image means to be the judge and arbiter of what is good and what is evil instead of being carriers of His breath - which is why "religious" people are so judgmental, they are trying to be godly as understood through the filter of the Lie.

Our choice was to define our identity by law rather than by relationship. And the Lie left us believing that spiritual ends could be achieved purely in the flesh. But because it left our human spirit compromised in its ability to receive from heaven, there was no way to correct the soul's perception and reshape it according to heaven's intentions.

We exchanged the Truth for a Lie, Love for Fear and Fruit for Famine. And we crushed out spirits under layers of flesh.

By now I'm sure you can see why the supra-natural life requires us to encounter:

• Words of Truth to undermine the Lie

- Words of Love to cast out Fear
- Words of Favour to replace the Famine

God needs to re-form the soul, to redeem every experience that was shaped by the Lie and to restore the full truth of who we were made to be. And this, as we shall see in the next chapter, is exactly what Jesus taught His disciples.

His Word of Grace Over You

Before we look at what Jesus taught His disciples I would like you to take some time with Father, asking Him to speak over you. You may feel awkward about this. Even those who believe Jesus still speaks today have often left hearing Him to the "professionals" and so are not very practiced. But without the ability to hear heaven we cannot be what we have been made to be.

"...to listen is better than the fat of rams." (1 Samuel 15:22)

In other words, the practice of listening is more effective in your walk with Father than all the sacrifices you make for Him and all the things you do for Him. The more we listen the more we will hear with understanding. When a child is newborn it doesn't understand the words being spoken to it by its parents, but the words still speak into its emotions, to soothe calm and comfort. In time, a child will start to get impressions from its parents' words and eventually it will understand them all. As it is in the natural, so it is in the supra-natural.

Take time listening to God. At first it may seem like you hear nothing you understand, but you feel His presence and comfort. Then you might start getting impressions of things. Eventually you will start hearing heaven with clarity.

Jesus says, *"No one comes to the Father except through me"* (John 14:6). So close your eyes now (or after reading these instructions) and focus on an image or idea of Jesus. Jesus calls Himself "the door" and "the good shepherd" (John 10:9-11). He is "the way" and lots of other ideas besides. Focussing our imaginations on an image or idea that represents Jesus helps us to tune our spirits in to Him. Once you have that image in your mind let Jesus lead you to the Father and then listen for what the Father is saying over you. Try and put words or images to any impressions you get and make a mental note of these images and words so you can record them later.

Sometimes people will "hear" negative statements in this type of exercise. More often than not these statements are coming out of our own pains and low expectations of God's love and approval of us. If you experience this, come back to the Father in your prayer, but this time ask yourself as you do, "If the Father really loved me, what would He be saying?"

Don't rush this exercise, but when you have finished, write down the things you "saw", "heard" and "felt" from the Father.

Endnotes:

1. The Greek word for "sanctified" is *hagiazo* and means to be set apart for holy use, to be purified, consecrated, mature, complete etc.

2. *Restoring the Kingdom* by Dr Andrew Walker.

3. I know a lot of readers will think this is a good thing and that we need to be careful what we let into us. This is true and Jesus warns against being infected by the leven of different types of people. But I now understand that we are supposed weigh "what" we receive from each other. If someone has received Jesus, the Holy Spirit lives in them and their testimony will always contain something we can benefit from.

4. There are various theological opinions on exactly how dead or damaged the human spirit is from birth and what the implications of that are for our ability to receive from the spirit realms and heaven in particular. My assumption is that however it got damaged, the practical effect of life before the indwelling of the Holy Spirit, is that the human spirit is a broken receiver. We receive poorly, but we do receive.

5. There is a strong relationship between our sense of our own story and our sense of identity. When Jesus enters our story we call it "testimony", which is why "testimony" is so powerful. It is the essence of the truth of who we are in Jesus; it is the redeemed you; and it is that redemption story that overcomes the devil (Revelation 12:11).

5: Jesus' Discipleship Programme

*"Press hard upon the word of testimony,[1] seal up the
law among my disciples."* (Isaiah 8:16)

It was growing up under my father's teaching that I first learned
how, in John's Gospel, Jesus highlights three hallmarks or distinc-
tives that mark and identify His disciples. However, it has only
been in the years since my toilet epiphany (see last chapter), or
perhaps I should call it "the revelation on john", that these verses
have really become effective in me.

It began when I noticed the connection between Jesus' hallmarks
of discipleship and His own growth in *wisdom, character* and *favour.* Jesus taught His disciples only what was true for Himself. He
expected that they needed to grow in the same three dimensions.
For reasons that will become apparent, I will often refer to these
dimensions or axes as the three legs on a stool or tri-pod.

First Jesus says,

*"If you **abide in My word, you really are My disciples** and you
shall **know the truth,** and the truth shall make you **free.**"* (John
8:31-32)

Remember, Jesus grew in wisdom and here He says that the entry requirement into His development programme ("if you really

are my disciples") is abiding in His word in such a way that we encounter *truth* that is liberating.

Not everything that is true is necessarily freeing, but it is a mark of Jesus' disciples that the truths they are discovering and the way they are discovering them are liberating emotionally, spiritually and physically. There is a key dimension to our growth that is all about how and what we think and how we apply our minds. If this leg is growing correctly, then it will make us free.

Words that describe the flavour of this leg might be: "Knowledge", "Understanding", "Wisdom" and "Truth" with an after taste of "Freedom".

Next Jesus tells them,

"As I have loved you, *you should also* **love each other**. *By this* **everyone shall know that you are My disciples**, *if you have love for each other."* (John 13:34-35)

Now that they were on the programme, Jesus' disciples were encountering His love and out of this experience, Jesus tells them to love others. Interpersonal behaviour shaped by and expressing love is the quality that outsiders will most obviously recognise on those who are on Jesus' programme ("by this everyone shall know that you are my disciples").

Of course, all Christians know that they are supposed to be loving, but as I pursued my journey into Jesus I started to notice that there was a distinct connection practically, scripturally and psychologically between our experience of either "love" or "fear" and the way we behave. Put simply, when we feel loved we behave better and when we feel afraid we behave badly. Within minutes of meeting someone you can tell whether the defining experiences of their lives have happened in a context of love or of fear. If it is love, there is an easy confidence that does not feel competitive or pushy. This is why I equate this leg with Jesus' own growth in character. There is a dimension of our growth that is all about the experience and expression of love, which people see in our character.

Words that describe the flavour of this leg might be: "Character", "Behaviour", "Attitude", "Motive", seasoned with "Love".

Finally Jesus says,

*"If you abide in Me, and My Words abide in you, you shall ask what you will, and **it shall be done** to you. In this My Father is glorified, that you **bear much fruit**, so you shall prove to be **My disciples**."* (John 15:7-8)

This time there is an encounter with Jesus Himself and Jesus words' are now deeply embedded in the disciple. The result is that the disciple is fruitful in the things for which they pray and it is proof that they are following Jesus ("prove to be my disciples").

Jesus, of course, *"grew in favour with God and men."* If you have a love-shaped character it is easy to see why you might have favour with men, but people recognised that Jesus also had favour with God. If you get what you ask for in prayer, most people would call you favoured by God. Fruit is the evidence of the grace that sticks to us as favour. So there is a dimension of our growth that is marked by increased spiritual authority, because prayer is the primary way we exercise authority, "on earth as it is in heaven".

Words that describe the flavour of this leg might be: "Authority", "Strength", "Favour", "Faith", all with a heavy bouquet of "Fruit".

Once you start seeing this pattern you find these three legs all over the Bible. For instance, Paul often refers to what we call the three graces: "Faith", "Hope" and "Love". To me it seems obvious that faith is a flavour of the *favour* leg, hope is a part of the *wisdom* leg (our hopes are the possibilities that keep us free inside) and love is a part of the *character* leg. Or as Paul writes to Timothy: *"For God didn't give us a spirit of fear, but of power* [favour], *love* [character], *and a sound mind* [wisdom]." (2 Tim 1:7).

Try this simple exercise before you go on. The passage that follows in a typical encouragement from Paul. See how many words and phrases you can spot that relate to the heart life legs we've been looking at: Wisdom, Character and Favour.

"... that you may be filled with the knowledge of His will in all spiritual wisdom and understanding, that you may walk worthily of the Lord, to please Him in all respects, bearing fruit in every good work, and increasing in the knowledge of God; strengthened with all power, according to the might of His glory, for all endurance and perseverance with joy." (Colossians 1:9b-11)

See this chapter's endnotes for answers.[2]

Stay With Me!

I had known this outline for years. It taught me that being a disciple of Jesus meant learning more truths, loving people better and seeing more answers to prayer. No problem!

But now that I was consciously looking for more authority in Jesus, I had developed a more open and dependent attitude and I had started to discover the power of an encounter with *words of grace* in the Holy Spirit, the type described at the beginning of the last chapter by Paul. Change was happening in and around me. I had started to see healings again and I was becoming more confident in my ability to hear Jesus. I had also stepped out in faith, taking redundancy from my work as an IT consultant, believing that I should be in full time ministry. Five months after leaving my job and just as the money ran out, I became the full time leader of the church we had joined when God called us out of London!

It was important to me that I was able to pass on what I had learnt, so I decided to run a year-long men's discipleship group. Before it started I talked to Jesus about what I should do with the twelve sessions I had.

As I prayed I remembered the three-fold outline of discipleship as I had learnt it from John via my father. Immediately, I noticed its connection with the statement about Jesus' growth in Luke 2. I realised that there was something here that was more than just a sermon outline. Then, I noticed something important about the context of Jesus' teaching to His disciples. You may have already noticed it. It is a little word that appears in two of the verses I have quoted above. It is the word "abide".

*"The one who says they **abide** in Him should also live the same way He lived."* (1 John 2:6)

This little word had become very important to me over the previous couple of years. It was the word I associated with the inner encounters I had been having that were changing me. It is the way I had been learning to let God's word of grace take root in me.

I could have run a discipleship programme based on teaching people true things. I could have passed on some behaviour management techniques to improve their characters and tell them they must be really nice to each other, while hoping that if we all prayed enough we would see some answers to prayer that would encourage us enough to feel God's favour. But...

Spiritual ends are not achievable purely in the flesh, even when we have judged the process to be good!

It was part of the Lie believed by Adam, as he took on the responsibility to be judge of good and evil, that led him to believe he could achieve a spiritual end by fleshly means.

Spiritual growth requires the Spirit's input. Jesus makes all of His comments about His disciples growth in the context of them "abiding" in His word, in His love and in Him.

The word "abide" is a translation of one of John's favourite words. In Greek the word is *meno*. It means "to wait, to remain, to stay, to dwell, to live in, to take time in."

"Meno" is used 120 time in the New Testament. 69 of those times it appears in John's writings. While the rest of the Bible uses "meno" in it's everyday sense (so Timothy and others "waited" for Paul in Troas, Acts 20:5), John uses "meno" as a spiritual metaphor 51 times. We abide in Jesus and He abides in us (John 15:4). His word abides in us and we abide in His words (John 8:31;15:7). The Spirit abides with us and in us (John 14:16,17). Jesus is in the Father and the Father abides in Jesus (John 14:10). The Father abides in us (1 John 2:24). We abide in His love (John 15:9,10). His joy abides in us (John 15:11). Truth abides in us (2 John 2). We abide in light not darkness (John 12:46). Eternal life abides in us (1 John 3:15). God's seed abides in us (1 John 3:9). We abide in His house (John 8:35).

For me, abiding had come to describe an encounter with Jesus. These encounters had lots of flavours. Some were gentle, some were stern, some were funny and some were dramatic. At first they felt unnecessary or indulgent and they could be exhausting as well as refreshing. Often, I didn't really understand the point of them and with some of them I wasn't even sure if it was Jesus or my imagination speaking! However, I had submitted my right to understand before I would follow when Jesus had challenged my pride, so I stuck with it and in time started to realise that I was changing.

As I prayed about the shape of the discipleship programme I was planning, I knew that I needed to teach people how to encounter Jesus and His words of grace in ways that would help them grow in three ways.

It was then that I had a picture of an old fashioned, three-legged milking stool and I remembered that the useful thing about three-legged stools is that they are very stable.

A Three-legged Stool is Very Stable

Mathematically speaking, there is a reason why a stool with three legs will almost always stand up, even if the legs are different lengths and the floor is uneven. The theory is that three points will always lie on a flat Euclidean plane. So with just three legs touching the ground at three points, a stool or table always feels like it's on a flat surface, which is why cameras are put on tripods. In the real world, of course, there are limits, but as long as the legs are roughly matched, a three-legged table or stool can be used on uneven, broken cobbles and it will not wobble. Add more legs and the furniture rocks and rolls like Elvis, as anyone who has ordered drinks at roadside taverna in the Algarve can tell you.

In seeing the picture of the milking stool it was clear to me why so often we stall or fall in our growth. While wisdom, character and favour do not have to be perfectly matched in us, if one area is too stunted or over developed with respect to the others we become unstable and unfit for purpose.

It seems that there are three legs to our souls, related to what and how we *think*, what and how we *feel* and what and how we *do*. Whether we feel tall or small in Jesus, our legs need to be roughly the same size. Our overall maturity in Jesus will be defined as much by the length of our shortest leg as it will be by our longest.

We all know the stories of ministries that exhibit remarkable favour and fruit, but then fail dramatically because of character issues or unwise choices. These are just the tip of an iceberg.

Closer to home, have you ever noticed how you can meet people who seem to *"know all mysteries and knowledge"* but whose characters *"don't have love"* (1 Corinthians 13:2), nor do they change the world around them? Then there are those who prophesy and perform miracles in Jesus' name, but they don't seem to really know Him and their personal lives seem a mess. Or there are those we call saints because of their gentle natures, but in truth they have become so stoical that they accept every illness and adversity as a gift to produce more patience, instead of seeing it as a work of the devil or an effect of sin that they have the authority to deal with.

If we do not allow the Spirit to grow and challenge all of who we are, not just the bits we enjoy and feel comfortable with, then our walk of faith will eventually stall and stagnate. When this happens my observations are:

- That love of truth and wisdom becomes dogma over doctrine and an idolisation of the mind and intellect

- That love of people becomes kind hearted indulgence and passive irrelevance
- That love of fruit and favour becomes addiction to power and position

On reflection, it is clear that whole denominations tend to express a preference for one of these three genuine spiritual legs. Baptists tend towards Wisdom and Truth, Methodists go for Character and Pentecostals love Favour.

Coming back to my discipleship group, my decision was made. I would spend a year with them addressing all three legs of the stool. We would do this by learning how to "abide" in Jesus, in His word and His love. So I looked to create space in each session for everyone to encounter Jesus through times of listening to heaven, personal meditation and prophetic prayer. In the end it wasn't a perfect year, but for those of you who were on it, I want to say I am so proud of you! You are now businessmen, professionals, student workers, church leaders, worship leaders and more. Most importantly, you are doing it all supra-naturally!

So here is the formula:

Be deliberate in asking heaven for words of grace that speak to all of who you are - words that will displace the Lie with the Truth, Fear with Love, and Famine with Fruit. Then take time to dwell or abide in what God is saying to you.

Most of us do this instinctively to a degree, but being deliberate about it has proved to work time and again. Since that original discipleship group I have incorporated the model into other programmes and I still live by it myself.

Get To Know Your Legs

I have highlighted a number of different qualities or flavours that go with each leg. Even the way I name the legs varies a bit depending on my focus. If I'm thinking about the effect that growth in each leg has on me I call them Wisdom, Character and Favour. But if I'm thinking about the encounter that grows each leg I call them Truth, Love and Fruit. I also mentioned that Paul's three graces seem to fit too: Hope, Love and Faith. There is also a rough connection between the Holy Spirit's work in us, on us and with us as well. The Spirit on us tends to reveal the truth of who we are, the Spirit in us manifests the love of God, and the Spirit with us demonstrates favour.

So why don't you create three columns and label them Wisdom, Character and Favour. Then make three lists of qualities or principles that you think should go with each leg. Some things might come naturally in threes, but they don't need to. I normally include "authority" in my list under Favour, but it has no equivalent in the other legs (well, not in my list any way).

When you've done that, talk to Jesus and see if you can find some verses that go in each column as well.

Which is your strongest or longest leg and which is your weakest or shortest?

We will return to this theme again in chapter 7, but first we need to explore exactly how we press hard into these testifying words so that God's instructions for our lives get fully sealed in us.[3]

Endnotes:

1. i.e. a word of revelation about God, therefore a word of grace.

2. I think there are 12 in all, 4 for each of the three legs. Wisdom: knowledge, wisdom, understanding, increasing in the knowledge of God; Character: walk worthily, endurance, perseverance, joy; Favour: bearing fruit, every good work, strengthened with all power, the might of his glory.

3. See verse quoted at the start of this chapter.

6: Heart Life

*"In the same way **the Spirit helps our weakness**; we don't know how to pray! So **the Spirit itself effectively intervenes¹ over and above² us** with groans that can't be spoken. And **searching our hearts, He knows what the mind of our spirit³ is**, because by God's charge He effectively intervenes on behalf of the saints, and we know that in everything, **He cooperates for good with those who love God**, who are called with a purpose ... to be conformed to the image of His Son."*
(Romans 8:26-29)⁴

I'm aware that this translation of these verses might surprise some, but it is legitimate one. It makes it very clear that it is our cooperation *with* the Spirit in all situations to bring about good that is the key to becoming like Jesus.

If you think carefully about the verses above you will also notice that the Spirit is active in us, on us and with us. Cooperation with the Holy Spirit is a foundation of the supra-natural life and the journey into Jesus.

God initiates, you cooperate!

This chapter is all about change in our inner lives: spirit, soul and mind - what a friend of mine calls *heart life*. The verses above come from the same passage in Romans that we have referenced several times already - the passage that concludes by setting a horizon for us go for, to be conformed to the image of Jesus. To get us there, the Holy Spirit is at work in our heart life. It was the quality of Caleb's spirit that fitted him to possess his promises in Canaan.

The Spirit In You

"I will put my Spirit within you, and cause you to walk in my ways, and you shall keep my judgments, and do them." (Ezekiel 36:27)

The renewal of our heart life starts when we receive salvation and God gives us His Spirit. The only cooperation required from us at this point is to receive Jesus. The renewal of our soul takes longer, but we'll come to that.

The human spirit was supposed to be like a radio or television aerial, capable of tuning into the music and broadcasts of heaven. In our fallen-ness it has become broken. While still capable of picking up signals, the tuning is unreliable and we can't be sure whether the station we are listening to is legitimate or an illegal broadcast. God, of course, is quite capable of speaking directly into even a badly broken human spirit. But for whatever reason, it seems Father would rather we had "ears to hear" than that He had to shout loudly and slowly at us all the time.

When we get "born again" it as if we had a new back-up spirit put in along side our old human spirit. This one is the Spirit of God, but God's Spirit now incorporates the human spirit that Jesus had. I guess if the Holy Spirit didn't include this full human spirit He could not have come and remained in us without overriding our humanity. The human body would have simply become an avatar of Yahweh with no real freedom or contribution to make. This is why the Spirit couldn't be given until Jesus had completed a full human life. Here is something new under the sun and in God. It is the "Holy Spirit incorporating the spirit of a fully victorious human". Lets call it the "HS/MAN+" component and push the electronics analogy a bit further.

The HS/MAN+ fits into us like the original component (the S/MAN1.0) so nothing else needs changing at this point. I have a computer science degree and there was a time when I used build and modify my own PCs. I remember that back in the 90's, Intel brought out a chip upgrade that literally fitted over the older chip. Sometimes I imagine the HS/MAN+ fitting over the old S/MAN1.0. I don't know if the new one fixes the old, or if instead it just provides what is lacking or broken to complement it, or perhaps it totally overrides the old? My instinct says that whether instantly or over time our old human spirit is transformed or incorporated into the new rather than abandoned as redundant. To me this seems to be part of the redemptive nature of the work of Christ being formed in us.

The detailed mechanics of *how* the Spirit operates in us are less important than the work He does in us. Now with a working receiver on the inside, our inner lives start to hear the healing, guiding, empowering sounds of heaven. We start to clearly hear God's word of grace and we are changed by this, even when we do not understand what is being said. The word of grace being picked up, even if barely consciously, is dripping with tonic for the soul, but there are parts of who we are that require a more specific and targeted treatment. Which is why we must learn to hear with understanding.

If we do learn to hear God with understanding, then we can better abide in His word and start to cooperate with the Holy Spirit until His word abides in us. Entry onto Jesus' discipleship programme was learning to abide *"in his word"* (John 8:31). Graduation is demonstrated by the fruit that proves that His word *"abides in us"* (John 15:7).

Once a word from Jesus is abiding in us, part of our soul has been re-shaped and received a new experience to replace, heal or redeem one accreted in the days of our separation from God. The soul starts to be transformed and we are pleasing God by responding in faith to the word of Christ (Hebrews 11:6; Romans 10:17).

Replacing The Stony Heart

"I will also give you a new heart, and I will put a new spirit within you; and I will take away the stony heart out of your flesh, and I will give you a heart of flesh." (Ezekiel 36:26)

If God can give you a new spirit instantly why can't He just give you your new heart/soul at the same time? The answer is similar to the reason that Jesus had to live a whole human life before the Holy Spirit could be permanently breathed into mankind. Just as your humanity would have been annihilated by the in-dwelling of the unprocessed, raw Holy Spirit, your personal integrity would be destroyed if your soul was instantly changed. There are parts of your soul that have been laid down over time, through a process of experience filtered and processed through who you are already.

If the Father where to change your soul instantly, you would be new! But you wouldn't be a new you!

You see, your soul is what carries your story. Your past can be re-shaped, but it can't be replaced. God doesn't change the events of your past, He changes their meaning!

Two days ago I was discussing favourite science fiction novels with my son, Joel. We both ranked a novel by Iain M Banks in about fourth place. (I will not mention which one in case you ever read it). This particular book has the most astounding surprise in the last few pages, delivered with total understatement. In just a few words of exchange between two characters, a single fact is revealed which totally changes the story just read. Emotionally you are just winding down from a powerful and intense story when you discover that the meaning of everything that you have just read has dramatically changed. The events are the same, but the new information has re-written their meaning. This is what the Holy Spirit wants to do in us, to turn our stories into testimonies. Your testimony is not just about "how you became a Christian", it is about how every part of who you are has been shaped or re-shaped by heaven. And He needs you to co-operate because, by definition, there are parts of your soul that you are responsible for.

God can't contradict Himself (2 Timothy 2:13). By nature God is rational. He doesn't act irrationally. Even if His ways are higher than ours and we don't understand them, they are still consistent with His faithfulness, love and justice. Which means that at one level[5], God can't make a genuine £1 coin! He can make a copy so perfect you would never be caught spending it, but by definition a genuine £1 coin is made by the Royal Mint, not God. If God were to make a genuine £1 coin He would have to re-write the laws of logic or world history and economics. He would be undoing things that He has already been involved in and, therefore, be denying Himself!

And so it is with our souls. There are parts of us that we are responsible for. So God acts consistently with His previous choices in making humanity and looks to empower and lead our hearts through His in-dwelling Spirit and His words of grace over us. To some degree, at least, if you've said "yes to Jesus" you are cooperating with this process, so eventually you will be fully redeemed. Our hearts will be 100% His.

*"For the eyes of the Lord search to and fro throughout the whole earth, **to show Himself strong in those whose hearts are completely His.**"* (2 Chronicles 16:9)

The greater the extent to which your soul or heart life has been redeemed, the greater the strength the Lord can reveal in you! The more the story carried in your soul is reshaped by the victorious Spirit that now lives in you, the more the grace of God poured out on you is carried forward as favour in you. Every event that has shaped you through your flesh can be given a new meaning and purpose by the Spirit's release of the truth and love of heaven. **The true spiritual authority we carry is not based on our competency of head or hand at a task, but in the heart victories we have won on our journey.**

Jesus was proved worthy of all honour and power not by His successful evangelistic campaigns and feeding programmes, but by maintaining a right relationship in His heart as He experienced the outrage of the cross. The sin in Adam's heart made him hide from the Father, but it was the sins of the world that hid the Father from Jesus' heart. Yet *His heart* never stopped loving, hoping and having faith. Jesus won the ultimate heart victory in His physical defeat.

So there is a process of redemption, as the victory of the cross that now lives in us is extended to every part of who we are. Whether an event in your past was a physical defeat or victory is irrelevant. Our history still lives in us and Jesus wants to give us a heart victory in all things. Where we've been wronged He wants to lead us into the victory of forgiveness. Where we've wronged others He wants to lead us into the victory of confession, which releases the ability to love in us. Where we have succeeded and done well He wants to lead us into the victory of thankfulness which leads us into His courts.

As I wrote this paragraph I found myself re-inventing some lines from Rudyard Kipling's poem "If". I'll put the lines in here. Sometimes rhyme can help us to remember truth:

If in your heart, Jesus is the master,
Then in your hist'ry victory will reign,
So whether life's a Triumph or Disaster
You'll treat those two imposters just the same!
If you can fill each unforgiving minute
With sixty seconds worth of loving done
Yours is the Promised Land and all that's in it
And what is more you'll be just like My Son.

Of course, none of this means that the process has to be slow. I often find that big steps forward happen almost in an instant with a new revelation. "Just one touch from the King changes every-thing".[6]

Redeeming History, Releasing Testimony

"I reckon that the sufferings of this current season are not worth com-paring with the glory which is about to be revealed in us." (Romans 8:18)

In recent years there has been a re-discovery of the power of testimony. In the telling of the stories of what Jesus has done in someone's life there is a release of faith in the hearers. But there is also a release of power from the testifier into the spiritual atmos-phere around them. There is a very real connection between what Paul refers to above as the "sufferings of this current season" and the "glory which is about to be revealed in us". The two things are not dislocated, separate events. The glory in us is revealed by the victory of Jesus redeeming the events that have shaped our souls. I know from experience that it is a fantastic thing for Jesus to redeem your past. However, as in the physical world, the healing or redemptive process can be more painful than the events that caused the damage in the first place. Crucially though, it is a dif-ferent type of pain. It is a pain that is giving birth to new life.

Redeeming The Bad

You may have a powerful conversion testimony. I know people who have lived through earthly versions of hell, physical and mental abuse, dysfunctional childhoods, occult and drug-soaked adolescence. But then Jesus has saved them and turned their life around. It is not unusual for people with this sort of testimony to develop an authority in ministry to others with similar backgrounds. Jesus has redeemed their life story, giving even the worst events meaning, value and power.

Jesus is such a good redeemer that sometimes people make the mistake of believing He must have caused the bad things to happen to them in the first place. Their authority and identity are so tied up with the events that Jesus rescued them from, that they feel these events must have been His will for them all along. But this is not the case. *"God is light and in Him there is no darkness at all."* (1 John 1:5).

My cancer is an integral part of my testimony and in one sense I am the person I am today because of it. But I know that Jesus didn't give me the cancer. He spoke to me quite clearly about this from the story of Joseph, where Joseph says to his brothers,

"You worked together evil against me, but God worked it together[7] for good, to bring about this day, to preserve many people alive." (Genesis 50:20)

God worked the evil plans of Joseph's brothers into His own plans for Joseph, but He was not the source of their evil plans. If you read the Joseph story you will also notice that Joseph had his part to play in cooperating with God and winning heart victories in the face of his ill treatment and unjust circumstances.

We all need transformation, even when our backgrounds were relatively normal and we seem like decent people. Some of us may be better equipped than others at managing or hiding the bad stuff in us, but it's there nonetheless. After we receive Jesus, we will probably try even harder at doing the right thing and using our natural skills to manage and hide the worst of who we are. But keeping a set of rules does not make us "good" - it can only ever make us a success or failure at the game of religion. While we might keep our failures secret and parade our successes, we know that sin still has power in us. Our hypocrisy is the hat that our vices doff to virtue. Sadly, many Christians happily accept management of their sins as a substitute for the redemption of the brokenness sin has caused in them. The first solution copes with life, the second carries favour and demonstrates the victory of Jesus.

To redeem the bad, Jesus often has to take us back into the pain, disorder and injustice that shaped it. To change its meaning He has to show us where He was in it all, what He felt about it and how He can turn it around for good. This is often uncomfortable. **But when He does it, the suffering is not worth comparing with the glory He is going to reveal in us.**

Redeeming The Good

We should not make the mistake of believing that power is only found in the dramatic testimony, or that Jesus is only interested in redeeming these big areas of damage in us. One of the reasons I believe so many fail to step into a mature authority in Jesus is because they do not realise that there are things in us that look "good" but are the fleshly imitations of spiritual fruit. *"For what ever doesn't come out of faith is sin"* (Romans 14:23). As we know, "faith comes by hearing, and hearing by the word of God". Doing good does not make you good! If good behaviour flows out of a part of our soul that has not been shaped by cooperation with the word of God, then according to Paul, it is not from faith so it is an expression of sin!

There is a lovely image from the life of Elisha. Some men come to him and say, *"Look, as my lord sees, the situation of this town is good, but the water is bad and the land is unfruitful"* (2 Kings 2:19). Elisha releases a prophetic word and action and the waters are "healed". Life can look like it's together on the outside - the "situation ... is good" - but without the word of grace there is something wrong in the "water" and the fruit of favour that proves we are carrying God's grace is not there.

A "bad" person can do "good" things for many reasons: fear of the consequences, desire for a reward, a need for love and connection etc. But a good person does good because that is their nature. This change of heart is something the Bible is clear can only be achieved by the Spirit in us, not by keeping a moral code (though keeping a moral code is better than living amorally). It is the difference between living by Law and living by Faith.

So Jesus also needs to redeem the good things that have happened to us and the good gifts we have in our natural abilities. Jesus says, *"Blessed are the poor in spirit, theirs is the Kingdom of Heaven"* (Matthew 5:3). It is often easier to rely on heaven for the things we know we don't have than it is to rely on heaven for what we are naturally strong in. The "poor in spirit" know that they don't have it in the natural to be blessed and so find it easier to access supra-natural blessing.

That is why Jesus says it requires God's help for a rich man to enter the kingdom (Mark 10:25-27). Jesus needs to redeem the good gifts and experiences that have made us naturally strong. This doesn't mean that He wants you to give up your gifts and benefits, but He often needs to untangle our sense of identity and security from them.

You'll remember how in my rest room revelation, God's word to me was that I compared my strength in biblical understanding against other people's. By doing this, I had an excuse not to acknowledge that in other areas they had so much more of Christ formed in them than I did. Today my gifts give me huge personal pleasure and I use them in ministry, but (for most of the time at least) I listen to others now, eager to hear their victories without the filter of defensive judgment. Jesus has redeemed the good in me that was natural and made it supra-natural.

To redeem the good, Jesus often has to challenge our pride and complacency and sometimes He even has to challenge us in our identity and security.

But when He does the suffering is not worth comparing with the glory He is going to reveal in us.

Redeeming The Ugly

If there are good things that need redeeming as well as bad things that need redeeming, then we shouldn't be surprised that there are also ugly things in us that need redeeming - unless of course you've never seen the classic Clint Eastwood movie![8]

In my definitions, the difference between the bad and the ugly is the knowledge in us of the motive behind our behaviour. Sometimes we know that we are being selfish, angry, untruthful etc - there is a direct connection between a bad motive and the things we are doing. This is wrong and the Bible tells us we have a responsibility in this.

But there are also things that we do because we are selfish, angry, untruthful etc, but for which we do not see the connection between the condition of our heart and the motive in our activity. We don't see it because *"the heart is deceptive above all else"* (Jeremiah 17:9). This is the ugly: the ways of behaving and thinking which we believe are fine; the things we put down to the way we are, but which can be destructive both to us and to those around us.

"If people experience me negatively, it must be their fault," we think, "because there wasn't any bad motive in my actions."

Sometimes, it really is other people's problem. There was nothing wrong with God in the garden, but sin in Adam made him experience God negatively. But perhaps it is the other person's fault less often than we think.

Have you noticed how there are some people for whom the same patterns of interpersonal breakdown or failure occur over and over again? I put this question in terms of other people, because it is always so easy to see in them!

That's because **we judge others by their actions, but we judge ourselves by our motives!**

We don't see how the way *we* talk, act and judge is reproducing the same bitter fruit everywhere we go. We weren't trying to upset people, make them feel small, imply we didn't value them etc, but there is something ugly in us that others experience while we do not.

When it comes to the ugly in us, fortunately grace and love cover a multitude of sins! The Bible tells us that while we do not have an immediate responsibility for these things, we are not exonerated by our ignorance.

"I know of nothing against me, but I am not acquitted by this, he who examines me is the Lord. So condemn nothing ahead of time, until the Lord comes, who will both bring to light the hidden things of darkness, and reveal the purposes of the hearts." (1 Corinthians 4:4)

Jesus doesn't condemn us for what is ugly in us. In fact, on the cross He has taken responsibility for it. It is His role to remove every spot, wrinkle and blemish from His bride (Ephesians 5:27). However, at the right time He will reveal our ugliness to us. By experience I know that as I have been deliberate in putting on Christ (Romans 13:14), He has come to me and brought the ugly hidden things to light, *"that he might purify and cleanse with the washing of water by the word"* (Ephesians 5:26).

To search out the ugly without revelation would not be good. We might discover truth, but it would not be truth that made us free, it would be truth that locked us up in shame. However, like Paul we should not believe that these things are not in us and we should be very open to Jesus putting His finger on them as part of His redeeming of our souls. If you deliberately avoid times of reflection it might be because deep down you already know the mirror is going to show you something unpleasant. So let light into a dark room and don't be surprised if you discover it is not as clean as you thought it was.

"I say to all, through grace ... do not to think of yourself more highly than you ought to think; but think clearly, with the level of faith God has given to each." (Romans 12:3)

"Those He loves he disciplines." (Hebrews 12:6; Proverbs 3:12)
Father knows when we are ready for truth that is not pleasant and if we are being transformed by Him we need to be prepared for some uncomfortable revelations. Once we have that revelation, the *ugly* in us has now become the *bad,* because we can now see the connection between our heart life and our actions. We now have responsibility with Jesus for the ugly, but because revelation is a word of grace, we will always have the resources we need to deal with what it reveals, even if we don't feel like we do.

The deeper we let His words of truth, love and favour go, the more ready we are to face the ugly truth in us and turn it into a testimony that extends and honours the victory of Jesus!

Every Christian will have experienced the things I am describing to some degree. There is a common manifestation of the Lord revealing the ugly in us; it is the experience of feeling "more guilty" about some things than we did before we were Christians. We need to learn early on in our Christian lives that the feeling of separation caused by our awareness of sin does not alter the fact of His indwelling commitment to us. There is no contradiction between the facts that we are fearfully and wonderfully made, that we are worth the life of the Son of God and the Father declares us righteous, and the fact that we are very broken.

If we are still trying to feel valued by our achievements then knowledge of our sin still makes us feel far from God.

Last year, the Lord spoke to me in perhaps the most unambiguous and specific way He has ever done. I'm not going to share the details as some things will remain private, but the consequences were like having the lid peeled off a can of worms in my heart. Ugly things that I did not know were in me suddenly became so clear to me I wondered how my heart could have deceived me for so many years. I felt like I should no longer be in ministry as I was confronted with the full extent and consequence of what I had excused as minor issues in me. But Jesus was very clear with me. The only difference between the day after this revelation and the day before it, was that I was now seeing what Jesus had known about and been covering in me for years! He had been able to use me despite these things to release healing, words of prophecy and encouragement, and to feed people spiritually. In all of this, Jesus had seen the worst of me and still loved me.

You might ask if Jesus could use me anyway. Why did He need to show me the ugly? All I can say is that in doing this Jesus transformed my pride, not into shame, but into a deeper love and appreciation for Him and for those around me: *"forgiven a little, love a little"* (Luke 7:47).

When the world challenges pride in someone, it is often to make them feel smaller so that they can be controlled more easily. When Jesus undermines pride in us, it is to release us into a deeper experience of love. Those who have been brought up as Christians often struggle in these kinds of areas simply because we honestly feel that there is not that much in us that needs forgiving. But the resulting silent pride robs us of the depths of love.

In redeeming the ugly in us Jesus may reveal things about us that shock us and rock us.

But when He does, the suffering is not worth comparing with the glory He is going to reveal in us.

The Person and The Persona

When Adam ate the fruit he became the judge of the good and the bad. But something in him became ugly too and it needed to be hidden. So he made clothes and hid himself among the trees, the same trees that God had given him as gift and which God had declared as "good" back in chapter 1 of the Bible. The ugliness in us needs to be covered. So a real person starts to create and project a persona to protect themselves from feeling shame and to give them a sense of value by clothing themselves in what the world at large or even God has said is "good".

The sinful man needs a moral code to hide behind. Even mafia murderers have their honour codes. The secular political class has a politically correct agenda to keep to demonstrate to the world that it is still moral. Political dictators are not bad in their own eyes, they are bravely doing what needs to be done for a higher principle, to refute capitalism or colonialism. Layer by layer the soul is smothered by the carefully constructed self-vindicating persona until the "heart is deceptive above all things".

"We are so accustomed to disguise ourselves to others, that in the end, we become disguised to ourselves."[9]

From the moment we become aware of the bad in us we start to construct our own personal persona to protect the "real" us from exposure and to tell the world how comparatively great we are compared with other people. Ironically, our persona actually obscures the beauty in us as well as the ugly. The persona might include the clothes we wear, the music we "like", the causes we sign up to, etc. But most subtly there are layers of this persona that exist in the narratives we create to vindicate ourselves as good wherever possible.

"And the man said, that woman that you gave me, she made[10] *me eat from the tree."* (Genesis 3:12)

I often wonder how history would have developed had Adam just said, "I was ashamed of myself, because I did something you told me not to do." But instead he created a version of events that blamed Eve and blamed God. Adam denied his need for grace and forgiveness and as a result he didn't receive it, even though God is slow to anger and rich in mercy (Psalm 103:8). Jesus came to redeem the *real you*, not your persona. To do this He needs us to stop hiding behind the stories we have created to make us look good, make us feel better, and make it all someone else's fault. He needs us to be real with Him.

Cooperating with Transformation Revelation

Looking back on the encounter I had with Jesus when I had cancer, I know it was due in part to an authenticity in me that was born of fear. In my room my façade dropped and anger, confusion and fear were poured out and thrown at my Maker. To have not been angry at Father would have been fake and He knew what I felt inside anyway. But in removing the veneer of religious propriety, we became close even as I thrashed out at Him. Like a child in hysterics, as my struggle waned, I found myself exhausted but in Father's arms. This is so much healthier than the child who stays polite on the outside, then sulks and nurses a grievance in the privacy of his/her own room.

To let Jesus redeem us fully we need to be as real with Him as we can be. We know that even when we hide our sin He knows about it. But we still hide it, because we have got used to playing a game with other people. A game where we accept their excuses even though we suspect they are not true and in return we expect them to accept ours without query. And so we expect God to play by the same rules. If we can give Him a convincing reason why it wasn't really our fault, we expect him not to challenge our version of events.

In playing this game we are missing out on intimacy and we are denying ourselves the opportunity for the deepest level of transformation, the formation of love, not as a choice, not as an action, but as the foundation of our being.

"So I say to you, her sins, which are many, are forgiven, for she loved much. But the one who is forgiven a little, loves a little." (Luke 7:47)

Jesus makes a direct connection between how much we love and how much we have been forgiven. If you read the verse carefully, you'll notice you can't say which came first, the love or the forgiveness. Like the chicken and the egg, the two are interwoven. You can't really receive love while pretending to be someone you are not. To really receive we must drop the pretence and admit who we are. To really know forgiveness releases love in us. Real love looks on the worst in us and goes on loving, selfish pseudo-love only wants only the best bits. We expect pseudo-love because that's what we tend to give other people. But Jesus is incredible in His love for us.

Sins used to temporarily separate me from the presence of Jesus. It felt that if I could just put a few days between a moral failure and my next deep conversation with Jesus, then we could just give the failure a quick acknowledgment and move on. But now my failures push me into Jesus' arms all the more quickly. I know that I can't transform myself, so while a failure is fresh in my mind I want talk to Him about it. I talk about the needs, fears, insecurities, rebellions and stubbornness in me that make me do what I do. I am not trying to excuse myself, but I want to give Jesus permission to challenge the roots of my ugliness not just it's fruits.

This is the power of confession at work. Confession is not a religious thing to do, it is an integral part of an authentic relationship. It gives permission to Jesus to change us by speaking words of grace into the areas of our lives that most need it. A lot of the time we simply need to become more authentic with Jesus. There are some areas in us that we know need changing and we are happy to tell Jesus this, but we don't tell Him that we actually like our sins and are not that bothered nor sorry about them. We just regret the fact that they seem to be on a list somewhere of things we shouldn't do. St Augustine once famously prayed, "Lord make me chaste, but not yet." We need to be authentic with Jesus about our misshaped emotions and desires. There are unhealthy thought patterns we indulge because we like them; there are people who in reality we don't want to forgive and probably can't; there are habits in our lifestyles which give us a sense of being different or help us fit in and we don't want to change them. If we start to talk to Jesus about these realities in us and invite Him to speak back, we give Him implicit consent to challenge and change us.

Sometimes Jesus' words of grace to us will be to challenge us to accountability with someone else: *"Confess your sins to one another"* (James 5:16). There is power in prayerful agreement with others, but the best kind of person to stand with you in confession is someone who has this attitude themselves. Jesus says, *"remove the plank from your own eye, then you can see clearly to remove the speck from your brother's eye"* (Matthew 7:5). Someone who is not open to their own transformation is not going to be an effective help to you. We often put off confession because we have experienced people who have used it as a control mechanism, but in an open and honest relationship it is a powerful tool for sealing the fruit of God's grace in our hearts.

The Power of Testimony

So layer by layer Jesus will peel off the persona to release the real person. He will replace what is now a "persona non grata" with a prophetic vision of who you were made to be, and step by step He will start walking you into this truth. Peeling off the persona is not comfortable. Over the years we have found our sense of security and identity in it and it will be a challenge to let go of it. **But the suffering is not worth comparing with the glory He is going to reveal in us!**

The upward call of God does not require us to try harder, though it does require us to be braver!

Fortunately, "boldness" is something the Holy Spirit is well known for bringing when He comes on us.

There is much more that could be written about the redemption process from these last two chapters. But it is the Holy Spirit who leads us into truth and there should be enough information here for the Spirit to turn into "seeds" of revelation and produce more fruit in your own heart-life transformation. The key is not a technique nor a programme, it is intimacy with God, Father, Son and Holy Spirit. In the next chapter we will connect these last two chapters by looking at how words of Truth, Love and Favour, transform the good, the bad and the ugly in us into testimony.

Opening Up

Before going on to the next chapter let's do a bit of confessing to Jesus - not as a religious formula, but as a dialogue in which Jesus can talk back to you as you uncover the real you. By all means be sorry, but don't whine and moan at God about your failure. Instead, be mature and honest reminding Him that He took on the responsibility to change you and you can only cooperate. So ask Him what you need to do to release His change in you. This is totally different from trying harder to not do the things you know you shouldn't do.

Do this with pen and paper and note things down as they come to you. You can re-visit these notes in a couple of days, months even years, and talk them through again with Jesus to see if they still make sense or to thank Him for the breakthrough He has given you!

Endnotes:

1. The Greek word *"entugchano"* translated "intervenes" or "intercedes" in English has a root that is about producing a result: *"teucho"*, meaning "to bring to pass", so the intervention is effective not just procedural.

2. The Greek word *"huper"*, from which we get the prefix "hyper", appears twice in this verse, once before and once after "effectively intervenes". Paul is really trying to get across that these interventions are beyond our own strengths and weaknesses.

3. In verse 27 I have taken the reference to the "spirit" to be the human spirit rather than the Holy Spirit, because the second appearance of the Holy Spirit as an object alongside the human heart makes for a confusing and logically strange sentence. Treating the word "spirit" as referring to the human spirit reads better and fits the flow of the argument better.

4. This is a significant departure in meaning from traditional translations that make "those who love God" passive with the Holy Spirit working everything together for their good. This is a much loved interpretation, but it is achieved by dropping the word "with" ("*sun*"), which is included in the Greek word for "cooperate" ("*sunergei*"), and replacing it with "for" or "to". Understanding "those who love God" as active co-labourers with the Holy Spirit both follows the flow of the previous verses and flows logically on to the next verse. For those who wish to explore this further I have included the Greek text for this verse from the "1624 Elzevir Textus Receptus" along with each word's translation in brackets, curly brackets have been used to group together the noun phrase "those who love God":
"*oidamen* (we know) *de* (also) *hoti* (that) *tois* (the ones) *agaposin* (who love) *ton* (the) *theon* (God) *panta* ((in) all things) *sunergei* (he co-operates with) *eis* (for the purpose of) *agathon* (good)."

5. Of course, at another level He has made every £1 coin ever minted! He created the raw materials and has been involved in guiding human history to the point that the £1 coin was invented.

6. *Just One Touch From the King* © Godfrey and Gill Birtil, Thank You Music.

7. The Hebrew word *"chashab"* translated here as "worked together", is used in the Bible in three main ways. Its literal meaning is "to plait, to weave or fabricate with different materials", so it is translated with phrases like "cunning skill" or "craftsman". It is also used in an accounting sense, working all the items into a single bottom line figure. Here it is translated "counted", "reckoned" etc. Finally, it used figuratively for the mental planning process and here it is translated "plotting", "devising" or sometimes just "thinking". The concept which covers all three uses is the idea of "working things together" which gives Genesis 50:20 a nice connection with Romans 8:28.

8. The Good, the Bad and the Ugly, a classic Italian "spaghetti western" film made in 1996 and directed by Sergio Leone.

9. Francois de la Roche Foucauld - French moral philosopher.

10. The Hebrew word *"nathan"* does naturally mean "give", but it has a causative aspect to it as well so I have translated it as "made", which conveys this sense and makes easier grammatical sense in English.

7: The Trinity in You

There is a trinity of grace in you.

- Grace in what and how we *think* produces Wisdom or Truth that Frees
- Grace in what and how we *feel* produces Character or Love that Shows
- Grace in what and how we *do* produces Favour or Fruit that Proves

Perhaps this is a reflection of the trinity in God's nature too. We talk about "the mind of Christ" and Jesus is God's Wisdom. We talk about the "Father heart of God" which reflects His Character. We talk of the "power of the Spirit" which is the foundation of Favour. A Trinity, by definition, means three distinct things that are impossible to untangle from a single whole. It is a Tri-Unity.

Have you ever noticed that while God is Father, Son and Holy Spirit, you can say Son of God and Spirit of God, but you never say Father of God. The Trinity is not a hierarchy, but there is priority: the Spirit and Son flow from the Father.

And so we read:

*"Even if I have the gift of prophecy, and **know all mysteries and all knowledge;** and even if I have **faith that removes mountains,** if I don't have **love,** I am nothing."* (1 Corinthians 13:2)

Here are the same three legs of the stool again, but love has a clear priority over knowledge (truth) and fruitful faith (favour). The priority of God's words of grace in us is the formation of Love. But this cannot happen without the formation of Truth and Favour simultaneously.

The Head, Doorman to the Heart

*"Take off the old 'you' which is being spoilt by the deceitfulness of desire. And be renewed in the spirit of your **mind.** Put on the new 'you', which is formed by God in the righteousness and holiness of **truth."*** (Ephesians 4:22b-24)

When it comes to how we actually experience change, Jesus often starts with Truth that Frees, then continues with Love that Shows, and ends with Fruit that Proves.

A revelation of *truth* produces a new *freedom* in me. The new *freedom* expresses Jesus' *love* for me, and so goes into me in a deeper way. Then I start to see the *fruit* of that revelation in results that flow from the things I do.

This is only a general rule, however. Sometimes, it is the *blessing* we experience on what we do that demonstrates Father's *love* to us, both as an experience for the heart and as a fact for the head.

Transformation often starts with a renewal of the mind because our minds act as doorkeepers at the entrance to our hearts, only letting in truth that conforms to what it deems appropriate. How we think determines whether we recognise a word of grace and how we will treat it. Will we let it in to our hearts? Will we abide in it until it abides in us? Someone who finds their identity in academia or intellectual pursuit may struggle to let grace into their heart, because grace doesn't always make sense to their head.

The renewal of the mind frequently starts with an encounter with truth. Jesus says truth comes from abiding in His word. This does not only mean Scripture. As I have previously explained, it was my pride in my biblical learning that needed to be challenged before I could be changed.

Jesus says that His sheep hear His voice directly and that we should live on what God says daily. He says that it is the Holy Spirit who leads us into *all truth*, in fact He calls the Holy Spirit the *"Spirit of Truth"* (John 16:13). A truth encounter may or may not involve the Bible, but it will always involve the Holy Spirit.

Wisdom: Truth That Frees

Truth changes us when it comes as revelation not information. Revelation is not the same as information. Information comes to us naturally, via the senses and intellect, whereas revelation comes via the Spirit. This book is full of what has been revelation for me, but second hand revelation is information until the Spirit of truth breathes life into it. We need to talk to Jesus about what we are learning naturally, letting the Spirit sift it and prioritise it. Information puffs up, revelation releases.

Revelation needs to be nurtured as it can be lost if we don't respond to it with faith. Faith starts with hearing, but is released with an action.

*"You see that faith was working in his works and **faith was completed by works.**"* (James 2:22)

It doesn't have to be a big action, but we should always do something when we hear from Jesus. The action seals and releases the power in "the word" far more than hearing alone. That is why I encourage you to write things down or confess them out. We co-operate with "the word" by our response to it.

God's words will challenge and change your perspective.

The challenge to change the way we think was actually one of

Jesus' core messages. "Repent" was Jesus' first and most regular sermon and "to repent" primarily means "to think differently". A change in behaviour may be a faith response or a consequence of the changed thinking, but the Greek the word for "repentance" actually means "perceiving beyond" or "beyond understanding"[1] rather than to change your behaviour.

Seeing the world differently is key to "repentance" as Jesus understood it. So He speaks about the affects of the "eye" on the way we live. In the modern world we often miss His meaning. The ancients looked at the eye and saw the patterns in the iris and the darkness in the pupil. They noticed the way these grew and shrunk and they also observed how different people could look at the same things and "see" totally different meanings and implications. So the iris and pupil became a metaphor for the patterns and ways in which we look at the world. When God calls us, *"the apple of His eye"* (Zechariah 2:8) He is saying that we are the filter through which He sees the world.

We all see the world through a filter. That filter, our eye, can be good or evil, filling us with light or darkness (Matthew 6:22-23). Jesus says our eye can *"scandalise"* or cause us to *"stumble"* (Matthew 5:29) and He says that we need to remove the planks and specks from our eyes to see clearly (Matthew 7:5).

Some people's filters are obvious. Someone who has experienced abandonment as a child may subsequently approach every new relationship looking for the signs of its failure. In doing so, they may create the very failure they are fearful of and in doing so endorse the very suspicion through which they view the world. However, we must be careful not to make the mistake of thinking that only certain people (perhaps those with difficult childhoods) have filters that unhelpfully distort the way they see the world. If, like me, you tend to see the world through those proverbial "rose-tinted spectacles" you are likely to be somewhat blind to the real pain and injustice around you. We all carry paradigms that the Holy Spirit has to help us see beyond.

Today, psychologists would say that those filters or paradigms are actually in the mind (the ancients knew this as well, but they also knew the power of a good metaphor). In fact a lot of psychology is built on this simple idea expressed in a simple equation:

$$S + T = B$$
(Situation + Thinking = Behaviour)

The way you behave is determined by the situation you are in and the way in which you think. But crucially, there is also a connection between the way we think and the different situations we find ourselves in. We adopt different modes of thinking based on context. My friends, Stephen and Mara Klemich, the couple who coined the phrase "Heart Life", taught me how to use this simple truth to initiate a dialogue with Jesus that would lead me into a word of grace.

Let me give you a simple example: I noticed that I behaved differently with my children's teachers than with other people. The difference was subtle, but I knew it was there. In fact, I treated teachers differently in school to the way I would treat them if they turned up as a stranger at church. As I started asking Jesus about this He showed me how I was behaving defensively and cynically because of my own experiences at school.

In my primary school, in particular, I had two teachers who treated me as stupid and bad. Partly as a result of this, something grew in me that meant by the age of 11, I became the first child at that school to be caned for misbehaviour. This was back in the day when a good thrashing was thought to do a child's constitution no end of good. My secondary school was much better and in many ways was a healing place, but I still got involved in an incident that burnt part of that school down. The Holy Spirit started to show me that there was anger in me triggered by schools and an expectation of being unfairly treated and judged. I didn't experience this as hot anger, rather I felt it more as a silent coldness which manifested in heart-protecting cynical behaviour. On the surface I would go through the motions of interacting with a teacher, but my heart was never going to connect with them. And you can't be a blessing to someone you won't let your heart connect to.

As I dialogued this with Jesus He started to remind me of the incidents that had developed my attitude and He showed me His heart for me in what had happened. He helped me to re-see the incidents with the perspective of an adult, which undermined the experiences I had had as a child - experiences that still lived in me as part of my soul. He also showed me other areas of life that triggered ways of thinking in me that prevented me really connecting with people. I was losing opportunity after opportunity to bless and be blessed because I saw others through the filters of my unredeemed past, not as Jesus saw them.

Of course, that past can also make some things look and feel good but for the wrong reasons. I realised that part of my love for church (something that seemed good) was actually a selfish desire for security and validation. I loved church because it was a situation where my Bible knowledge and healing testimony made me a teacher not a learner. But to be a blessing that had to change.

The truths I lived in with Jesus during this time changed me considerably. People in church now tell me I am so much easier to relate to than I used to be. It all started with an observation and an equation that led to revelation and transformation.

If "repent" primarily means to "think differently" it can sometimes be used to describe a change in lifestyle because, "Situation plus Thinking equals Behaviour"! So,

"Don't be conformed to this world, but be transformed by the renewing of your mind..." (Romans 12:3)

Truth needs to be prioritized by the Holy Spirit: Not all truth is equal. When asked, Jesus was happy to answer the question, *"Which is the most important commandment..."* (Mark 12:28).

While all Scripture is "God breathed", not all is equally important. Tithing garden herbs is good, but irrelevant if you don't live in the more important truths (Matthew 23:23). The Pharisees' inability to prioritise truth correctly was criticised by Jesus who observed that they where *"straining out gnats while drinking camels"* (Matthew 23:24).

We all prioritise truth and Scripture whether we realise it or not. Most Christians believe the same things, it's just we believe them in different orders. The order in which we believe things makes a huge difference to our experience of God. It could be the difference between being locked up under Law or being free to fly in the Spirit.

All truth is true, but some truths are truer that others!

We need the Holy Spirit not just to reveal truth to us, but to set truths in their right place. Let's consider a simple example:

It is true that God is a *Judge*. It is one of the most common things said about Him in the Old Testament. But it's also true that God is a *Father*, although the Old Testament only mentions this a handful of times. Jesus always referred to God as a father because He knew that God's fatherhood was a deeper truth than God's role as judge, even though both were true.

You can be a judge whether you are a father or not, but you can't be a father without needing to be a judge. Try taking a long journey with three young children in the back of a small car with a can of coke and you will see what I mean! Being a judge is a consequence of being a father. But being a father is not a consequence of being a judge.

Being a Father is in God's nature, but being a Judge is just His day job!

Truth that sets us free tends to be about who God is to us or who we are to Him. Jesus wants to show us who we are in Him, who He is in us, who we are today and who He has made us to become. It is part of the discovery of the eagle in you hidden under pigeon's clothing.

Strangely this revelation about who we are often comes when we are trying to see more clearly who Jesus is. As we see Him, whether in Scripture or in dialogue through the Spirit, He shows us who we are in Him and who He is in us.

For instance, Jesus asks Peter, "Who do you say I am?" Peter gives Jesus a rather obvious response in just ten words, but Jesus commends Peter for his revelation and then speaks over fifty words back to Peter, telling Peter who He is (Matthew 16:15-19). That seems a very generous return to me and is something I've experienced on a number of occasions.

Just last week I was in a worship meeting and I was totally focussed on myself. I was telling Jesus all the things that were bothering me and making me unhappy. Then I thought, "Hang on, this is supposed to be about Jesus," so I started telling Jesus why I loved Him. As I spoke out who He was for me, it was as though Jesus multiplied my words back to me. I found myself in convulsive holy laughter and filled with joy. Jesus doesn't have to speak English to tell you the truth of who you are to Him.

If you seek revelation about who Jesus is, you will discover who you are now and who you were made to be. In showing you this, Jesus is drawing your attention to the horizon and how to get there. He is moving the process of salvation on - a process that started with your freedom from your debt to sin, but is not completed until Christ is fully formed in you (Galatians 4:19).

The *head* often needs to be renewed first so that words of love will be let into the *heart* to further transform and redeem the soul. It is out of this heart victory that we often see the fruit of favour on the things we put our hands to. But fruit in the hand can itself be a word of grace to both the head and the heart, increasing our understanding and experience of love. The relationship between truth, love and fruit in us is not linear, but if truth clears the building site, love lays the foundation.

Character: Love That Shows

*"Don't grieve the Holy Spirit of God, in whom you are sealed for the day of redemption ... but be imitators of God, as dearly **loved** children; and walk in **love**, as Christ has **loved** you..."* (Ephesians 4:30-5:2a)

The experience and expression of love is the most important part of our transformation, but we often need to encounter truth before we can encounter love. Adam experienced fear in the presence of a loving God because he had believed a lie. To know love it is not surprising that the Holy Spirit has to clear away the misconceptions and lies. Encounters with truth are just the start of a process. A revelation of truth needs to lead us into an experience of love.

To have Christ formed in you is to have a heart life that has been shaped by the love of God.

In Proverbs we meet Jesus personified as God's wisdom, possessed by God from the beginning and anointed since eternity (Proverbs 8:22-23). Here, Jesus as Wisdom says:

"I was His delight every day, always laughing before him, laughing in the world, His earth. And my delight? The children of men!" (Proverbs 8:30-31)

This beautiful passage expresses creation as a joint project between Father and child as an expression of their shared love, and it tells us that Jesus has known His Father's delight and pleasure every day, and that now every day Jesus takes the same delight and pleasure in us. Because He was loved by the Father, Jesus loved us, and so He tells His disciples that it is out of their experience of His love that they will love others.

The truth of Jesus' constant delight in us is as true as the truth of the Father's constant delight in Jesus. But sin has disrupted our experience of His love over us. If we are going to become like Jesus then we need to step not just into the knowledge that He loves us but also into the experience of His love. Later on in Proverbs it says:

"Under three or four things the earth trembles, they're unbearable. **When a slave becomes a king...** *"* (Proverbs 30:21-22)

The sentiment is the same as we have already read in the book of Romans. Here the earth trembles, there creation groans. The reason for the world's anguish in both passages is that those with the right to reign are living out of their experience as slaves. Both Old and New Testaments recognise that if our emotions and ways of thinking have only been shaped by our years in slavery, then the earth around us is in for a very bad time.

This is exactly the situation in which the world finds itself. All of God's heirs have been released at some point from a slavery to sin. Fear, lack and control are the defining experiences of slavery. Love, provision and freedom should be the defining experiences of sons and daughters.

When we receive salvation we start to experience the Father's love and provision. While these experiences are fresh in our mind we tend to behave with more dignity, to expect more without being presumptuous: our character changes.

In the years directly after my healing and encounter with a loving Father God, my life did reflect the sort anticipated by Paul for those who love God. My character at school changed from being a people-pleasing hanger on, embarrassed by my "other life" at church, to a confident leader, comfortable enough in my relationship with Jesus that I didn't need to make others uncomfortable with it.[2]

On my first day back at school after my healing I was greeted with a mocking call of "skinhead" (I had lost all my hair on a cycle of chemotherapy). I turned and saw one of the "hard" kids who used to intimidate me. As I walked over to him I saw him bristle ready for a confrontation. I realised he didn't recognise me, so I simply pointed out he knew me and then told him what Jesus had done for me. I think I was more shocked by the change in my character than I had been by the healing in my body!

In my new confidence I found myself speaking in school assemblies and debates, sharing my faith with teachers as well as pupils, organising meetings and evangelistic events and inviting friends to them. I also found my prayers were effective. People would be filled with the Spirit as I prayed for them. I prayed for a man with a twisted spine and saw his leg grow out by a couple of inches (actually, I missed the growing as I had shut my eyes). I went on to university and saw more healings, deliverances, supernatural provisions and fillings with the Spirit. I also met Judith, who was to become my wife and best friend, a support, and gift from God to me.

Gradually as these new conversion experiences and blessings become memories, they blend in with all the other experiences of life.

And who we have been seems to swamp who we were becoming.

So we must prioritise the experiences of God's love and provision over the experiences and memories of life in the flesh, even when those fleshly experiences were good. We do this by being deliberate in pursuing His presence and love, by practicing thankfulness, by learning to celebrate His goodness in the face of injustice, by becoming certain in our hearts of who He has made us to be, and also by allowing Jesus to redeem our old life experiences, so there eventually becomes no part of us that has not be shaped by the love of heaven.

As our encounter with truth removes the blockages in our relationship with God, our perception of life will change and we will start to notice God's goodness around us and towards us. If our eye is good, our experience will change and we will feel His love in life's twists and turns.

We can help the Holy Spirit in this process by celebrating every experience of God's blessing and love to us by deliberately bringing thanks into our dialogues with Jesus and by asking and expecting Him to reveal His love through the events of each day. Simply feeling His presence and knowing He is speaking is enough to celebrate. The more intentional we are in letting our emotions respond to God's goodness, the more surely the experience of His goodness will become a part of who we are.

In this way we give the memory of blessing a higher priority in our souls than is carried by those memories shaped by our separation from God and our sin-filled environment.

John tells us that "perfect love cast out fear". As we become practiced at abiding in Jesus' love for us we will see the slavery in our hearts replaced by the *"glorious freedom of the Children of God"* (Romans 8:21).

Favour: Fruit That Proves

*"You were once shadow, but now you are light in the Lord. Walk as children of Light, seeing as the **fruit** of the Spirit is always in goodness, righteousness and truth. Proving what is pleasing to the Lord, have no part in unfruitful shady activity."* (Ephesians 5:8-11)

Fruit is the evidence of God's favour and pleasure on us. When Jesus says that fruit is the proof of discipleship, He says it in the middle of a passage that is full of John's favourite word, *meno* - to abide in, to soak in and take time in. Fruit comes because we are abiding in Him (John 15:5, 7) and in His love (John 15:9-10); He is abiding in us (John 15:5) and so is His word (John 15:7). It's interesting that to encounter truth we have dwelt in His word, but if we are experiencing fruit it is because His word now abides in us. Jesus also reinforces the fact that we are abiding in His love as He abides in the Father's love. It is as though *fruit* is the product of the previous encounters with *truth* and *love*.

But while this last area seems to be very clearly something that grows out of the other two, it still has a distinct life and growth of its own.

"Are you all apostles; prophets; teachers; or miracle workers? Do you all have gifts of healings? Do you all speak with various languages? Do you all interpret? **So zealously desire the best gifts.** *"* (1 Corinthians 12:29-31)

Just before reminding us that *love* is more foundational to us than power or knowledge (1 Corinthians 13:1-3), Paul tells us that if we are not yet operating in a ministry gift we should be zealous in desiring it. We can and should make the pursuit of the supernatural a part of our encounter dialogue with Jesus.

Gifts of Grace and Favour

As Paul continues, he says that he wished we all spoke in tongues and that we all prophesied. These two gifts express the foundations of the supra-natural life and the favour leg in particular. We shouldn't be surprised that there is a connection between "gifts" and "favour". In Greek they are both the same word - *charis*. The same word that we saw in chapter 2 translated as "grace" when it is given and "favour" when it's received, is translated as "gift" when it is the object being given.

Tongues:

The gift of tongues is a grace that when used privately, is all about our communion with God. It is a gift that helps us to abide in Him. Through tongues, the deepest parts of our being express themselves to the Father without the filters of our logical mind getting in the way - spirit speaks to Spirit. Tongues build up the inner life.

The gift of tongues is different to all the other spiritual gifts, in that it is given specifically to build up the individual. All the other gifts are given to build up the Church (1 Corinthians 14:4) or change the world outside us.

Prophecy is the foundational gift through which the power of our communion with God is released to change the outside world. Tongues open our hearts to the open heaven above us and lift us from our earthly circumstance into heavenly places. Prophecy receives the word of God and then acts on it.

Between these two gifts we see in embryo the entire spectrum of the supra-natural life. Which is why Paul wants everyone to have them.

I first spoke in tongues when I was sixteen, shortly after being healed from cancer.[3] At first I felt great about it, it made me feel loved by God and I used tongues in my prayer life without thinking about it. In my middle years I became a bit blasé about tongues. I used it in group prayer settings because everyone did and you have to let people know you can pray in tongues too! But in my private prayer I tended to "pray with my mind" which is a vital compliment to praying in tongues (1 Corinthians 14:15). I had a shopping list of things to pray for, so praying with my mind seemed more appropriate to praying in tongues.

Ironically, this is the exact opposite of what Paul encourages us to do. Paul who "spoke in tongues more than all of you" obviously did this in his private prayer life, because he tells us that while singing or praying in tongues in church is fine as worship, it doesn't engage the group, so if we are all together why not pray in a way the involves everyone.

Paul was not against public praying in tongues. His point is that the real purpose of tongues is the building up of the person praying. So Paul talks about praying with the mind only after he mentions praying in tongues! He expects us to lift our spirits into heaven through tongues before we start making requests or releasing faith through our prayers.

Perhaps it was because I had things the wrong way round that I became complacent about tongues in the same way that the Israelites became bored with the miracle of manna. Like the cherry on a Chelsea bun, tongues became a decoration I could take or leave. Today it is very different. Tongues sustain me throughout the day. I find myself quietly praying in tongues while I do all sorts of other things. My encounter times with Jesus almost always start with tongues.

Prophecy:

The gift of prophecy on the other hand was a grace I didn't step into until much later in my Christian walk. We will look at how to prophesy in the third book in this series. Prophecy is given to build up the Church. As a member of the Church, how you receive prophecy will determine what effect it has in you. Prophecy is simply a word of grace that has come to you via someone else.

Even before we are able to hear Jesus with clarity, He will speak to us through other people. Learning to nurture and let these words bear fruit in us is a part of the preparation for living in the words Jesus speaks directly to us. And even when we have learnt to hear Jesus for ourselves, Jesus will still choose to speak powerfully into us through other people. It is part of Jesus' plan to make us one body. We are never independent. We will always need each other to release, impart and prophesy us into the image of Jesus.

Tongues is the gift that helps us climb Jacob's ladder to get heaven's perspective. Prophecy is the gift that releases what we have seen whilst up there.

Gifts are the currency that change hands as grace becomes favour.

The interaction of faith working with fruit and favour is the dynamic by which the supra-natural life in us changes the world outside us. It is where we discover how to cooperate with the Spirit who is *with us*. A later book in this series will explore this dynamic in a lot more detail, but before we let the Favour leg grow too big we need to make sure that we know how to grow the Wisdom and Character legs of the soul too. This is simply because our unhealed human nature is normally far keener to change the world than it is to be changed itself. So this book has focused on the process of inner change, but the expectation is that: as the world in you is transformed you will see the world around you changing too. You will exercise more spiritual authority and you will have grown in favour with God and people.

Getting the Balance

Before we leave these three heart dimensions behind, a word of caution. Moses failed to enter the Promised Land not because he was not accomplished enough in his strength, but because he had failed to find grace for his weakness.[4]

When the Lord first called Moses, He made the shepherd's staff that Moses carried a symbol of His authority and God's power. Moses was comfortable with this - he had carried the staff for years. But when the Lord asked Moses to speak to Pharaoh, Moses said that he couldn't, because he was no good at speaking. God offered to Moses to, "be with your mouth and teach you", but Moses asked for someone else to do the talking instead. As a grace, the Lord gives Moses Aaron to do the speaking for him and extended His promise, *"I will be with your mouth and his mouth"* (Exodus 4:1-15).

Now fast forward to the end of Moses' ministry. God asks Moses to speak to a rock to release water from it. Still Moses will not "speak" and Aaron is now dead, so he falls back on what is comfortable and what he knows will work. He hits the rock with his staff. Moses gets the miracle, but the Lord tells him that because he hadn't obeyed God, Moses wouldn't enter the Promised Land (Numbers 20:7-12).

There is a tragically ironic postscript to the story. When Moses dies looking over the Jordan at the Promised Land he has never entered, the final editor of Deuteronomy observes, *"Moses the servant of the Lord, died in the land of Moab, by the mouth of the Lord"* (Deuteronomy 34:5). God had promised to be Moses' mouth for him because he was "slow of speech". God's little promise was ineffective in Moses and Moses never tasted the fullness of the bigger promise, Canaan.

We all have natural strengths and weaknesses. The Holy Spirit will cover our weaknesses and intervene effectively for us when we need it. But there is a cooperation that the Holy Spirit needs from us if we are to fulfil the purpose of our calling. If we only ever look to hone our strengths we will never learn to depend on the Lord to show Himself strong in us (2 Chronicles 16:9). The irony is that our weaknesses are not our limitations, they are actually our greatest opportunities, because, *"when I am weak, then I am strong"* (2 Corinthians 12:10)

It is not a question of addressing our weakness in the ways that motivational business management programmes encourage people to do. This is just fleshly behaviour management. Sadly, there is an awful lot of what passes for godliness in churches that is really just this. It's not that it is wrong or evil and it does have its uses, but it can become a substitute for real transformation. And it is the work of God in us that produces real authority and favour.

When we are unbalanced in our heart life a number of things might happen. Often the Father's grace over us seems to stop us growing at all and the Christian life can start to get frustrating. We have known real blessing and growth in one or two areas but suddenly we seem to have reached a limit. If Father needs or wants you to grow in a different way, then continuing to try and grow in the things you have already learnt in the Spirit risks messing them up with ideas that have come via the flesh.

Fortunately, I know from experience that Jesus is such a good re-deemer He will often sanctify what I try to achieve without Him. In my own desire to see more physical healing I read all sorts of books and memorised principles and verse lists, but these just left me confused and dependent on formulas. Actually, I needed to become better tuned to hearing Jesus and less fearful of looking foolish. As I relinquished my right to pride, my prophetic gift has grown in recent years. I have done and said some dumb things that have released the grace of God into a situation without fear of looking or sounding stupid! As I have grown in these other ways, all the things I had previously learnt naturally about healing have had the breath of revelation put on them by the Holy Spirit.

I have also had to go through the more painful process of undo-ing the mistakes I have made in striving to maintain growth where there wasn't grace. In some cases Father has even had to strip them off me. Father does discipline those whom He loves. In these situ-ations Father's grace is still on us, but it is there to do something different in us. We need to find out what it is and let Him lead us. Undoing what we have achieved in the flesh is not always a pleas-ant process.

On other occasions, Father's grace does let us grow unevenly and then fall over. But *"a righteous person falls and gets up seven times"* (Proverbs 24:16). The Lord knows what He is doing so as we dust ourselves off we try to learn the lessons of our fall.

It is our response in those moments when we seem to have stopped moving forward or have suffered an embarrassing failure that we make the choices that determine whether we will fully enter in to what we were made for or not. Do we walk away disil-lusioned or perhaps settle for stories of yesterday's manna? Or do we start looking to Jesus for revelation as to why we are stuck and what we need to do about it?

In these moments do we choose to fall back on the flesh or lean into the Spirit?

Abiding Time

Before we go on it is good to take some time to consolidate what we have been learning and let the Spirit breathe on it. Why not go back and note a few of the statements about truth that are highlighted in bold. Let them move from being information to revelation. It may mean you need to talk to God about them for a while.

I'm going to ask you to take a bit of abiding time in Jesus, to discuss your own development in the light of the model presented in this chapter. Abiding means to "take time", "to wait", so it would be good to start by simply opening your heart to Him. If you don't yet pray in tongues, now is a great time to start.

At its most basic level, tongues is a private language. As you grow in your gift you might start to notice a sort of vocabulary and grammar develop, but initially it is not unusual for tongues to be like the noises a child makes trying to imitate its parents' speech. Romans talks about the Holy Spirit praying inside us with *"groans too deep for words"* (Romans 8:23,26). So just try to let the work of the Spirit in you flow out of you towards heaven. Don't be too analytical. The deepest parts of who you are exist below the radar of your analytical faculties, which is why they can't express themselves in natural language.

Once you have spent some time engaging with Jesus start to talk to Him generally about each heart life axis we have been thinking about. Ask Jesus: "What am I strong in?" "What am I weak in?" What made you strong in a particular area? Can you see growth in all three axes over the last year? Are there axes where you are stuck? Do you need to give permission to Jesus to change you in some way?

Consider the following and write down anything you feel, hear or see.

- Ask Jesus to tell you something true about you
- Ask Jesus what he likes about you
- Ask Jesus what he wants to change in you

Endnotes:

1. Greek *"metanoeo"* is made up of "meta" which means "after", "beyond" or "behind" as in "Metatarsal", which is the bone beyond the tarsal bone, and a shortened form the word *"noieo"*, which means to "perceive", "understand" or "think". In English this is seen at the end of the word "paranoia".

2. There is a boldness in the Spirit that we can't know in the flesh. When we try to muster up courage, perhaps because we know we must witness, we often come over as badgering or desperate, neither of which really endorses the message we are trying to convey.

3. I actually had an experience when I was five that I now realise was tongues, but at the time I had no idea what I was doing. We were in a church that did not practice gifts, at least not publicly, so I had no context for what happened. Recently, I remembered the event and with hindsight it made sense.

4. I'm grateful to my friend Stephen Klemich for pointing this out to me.

8: And All the Rest

Jesus left His Church with two prophetic sacraments: Baptism, which prophesied a life continuously immersed in the Holy Spirit and Communion, which most importantly prophesied fellowship with God. These two principles, ritualised in the Church by immersion in water and the sharing of bread and wine, represent the foundational practices of the supra-natural Christian life.

The more we are deliberate in being immersed in the activity of the Holy Spirit, the easier communion becomes. And communion with God is a two-way conversation. The more God's words of grace have built me up, the more constant my daily dialogue has become. To *"pray without ceasing"* (1 Thessalonians 5:17), means to involve Him in every moment of the day, but it also includes dedicated times and seasons that are more about *being* with Him than *doing* for Him - which is why the Sabbath was so important in the Old Testament.

"So there remains a Sabbath rest for the people of God. For the one who has entered His rest has himself rested from his works, as God did from his." (Hebrews 4:10)

According to the book of Hebrews, the failure of the people led by Moses to enter the Promised Land was a failure to enter into God's rest (Hebrews 3:8-11).

God's rest is a place of fellowship, communion and intimacy. And entering into it means an end to works of Law. The fact that Law has no place in intimacy should be obvious. To bring up rights and requirements over an intimate meal with your spouse would kill the moment. Intimacy celebrates the intrinsic value of the partners to each other. It doesn't calculate balance sheets to see who owes what to whom.

That doesn't mean that intimacy does nothing. It is just that the things we do will be positive expressions of the relationship, not an attempt to create a relationship nor manipulate it. There is a way of thinking in some parts of the Church that believes that doing anything is somehow legalism. It believes that work was something that happened after the fall, when in truth God gave Adam a job to do in tending the garden and filling up and subduing the earth way before the snake ever spoke.

The "works" that the New Testament is so clear we need to stop doing are the ones that are trying to achieve a moral or spiritual objective without the Holy Spirit's input. That's why He is the "Holy Spirit" - there is nothing *holy* that He's not involved in and there's nothing *spiritual* that He has not breathed life into. And so as well as "works of law" there are "good works" which God has prepared for us to walk in (Ephesians 2:10) and these works release the goodness and purposes of heaven because the Holy Spirit does them with us. The heavenly purposes released by acts of faith include our growth and transformation, so if we fall into the trap of assuming we should do nothing we will not grow, because we will not do the things that by faith release the power of our communion.

An Easy Yoke!

In this final chapter I want to explore what it means to live free of the Law and in rest and intimacy. The New Testament says life lived free of the Law is led by the Spirit (Galatians 5:18) and walked out by faith (Romans 3:28). Most of us live with a mix in our lives. Some things we do by Law led by good intentions and some things we do by faith led by the Spirit.

At a basic level, Law is a good thing. Both Jesus and Paul endorse it. But it is a good thing that can't lead you into the Promised Land. Law can prevent the anger in my heart from murdering my neighbour, but it can't touch the anger in my heart. Law can constrain the actions of the covetous soul and stop it stealing, but it can't fill the emptiness that constantly desires more stuff to fill it.

Law is better than anarchy because it contains and limits the effects of sins in us, but Law can't make us good and it can't lead us into promise.

We can think about the stages of Israel's journey out of Egypt, through the desert and into Canaan as relating to the phases of slavery, friendship and sonship in the Christian's journey into Christ. In this model we can see that Law acts as a useful tutor during the wilderness period (Galatians 3:24) - a guide for the season when the Israelites knew what they had been freed from, but didn't yet see what they were freed for. In the wilderness people were living by Law, but they were also learning how to be led by the Spirit (the pillar of fire/cloud) and walk by faith as they responded to God words. The wilderness season was defined by this tension between faith and Law.

When you are a slave you have no choice in what you do, but once freed you do need guidance on how to make the right choices. God gave the Israelites the Law in the wilderness because without it the slavery still in their hearts would have really messed things up. Paul uses the fact that the Law was given in the wilderness very effectively in his argument against Law in Galatians. The Law was given at Sinai, which is not even in the Promised Land, thus proving that the Law was not God's final destination for His people and was only intended as a temporary measure until they reached maturity (Galatians 4:25). Thought of like this, it is easy to see how works of Law sneak into the practice of our faith. When someone becomes a Christian and joins a church they need to be given certain behavioural rules, because until Christ is adequately formed in them, their behaviour is unpredictable. While Jesus can handle their dysfunctional behaviour, churches often can't.

Church leadership has an authority to set rules. It is part of the binding and loosing that Jesus gives Peter authority in as the leader of the first church. And Paul regularly gave instructions to his churches on how to maintain community by sticking to agreed modes of behaviour. In different contexts these included how to dress, how, what and when to eat, how to celebrate communion and who could and couldn't teach. Paul always knew that these rules had nothing to do with the process of the salvation of the individual. They were simply the pragmatics of creating a community of unity from diversity.

All communities have rules of behaviour that hold them together. When everyone knows these rules instinctively they do not need to be written down. In a church that is seeing people come into it from all kinds of backgrounds and behaviour patterns there needs to be more intentionality about how they *"preserve the unity of the Spirit and the bond of peace"* (Ephesians 4:3). Some churches will need more explicit rules than others and different churches in different contexts will have different codes of conduct. This is healthy and normal. It need have nothing to do with Law unless we start to see our community norms as a signpost or catalyst to salvation.

Problems only arise because we fail to learn how to be led by the Spirit and walk by faith. Without this dynamic, all that we now know of the Christian life is the rules that hold our churches together, many of which will be justified and endorsed by Scriptures and even "common sense". But in common with all Law they still will not make you righteous.

The Israelites should have remembered the wilderness as the time when they learnt how to *"live by every word that proceeded from the mouth of God"* (Deuteronomy 8:3); as a time when they were led by His presence. They should have remembered how they thrived when they did what He told them to do. But they never learned these lessons. Instead they celebrated the fact that they had been given the Law to live by.

You see, no matter how hard a set of rules seems to be when you first start to live by it, once you have cracked a part of it at least it becomes the safe and lazy option. While others may struggle with it, we can feel good about what for us is now a well-ingrained behaviour pattern. It is interesting to note how the religious spirit is always very vocal in upholding the rules it is never likely to break! There is something comforting about a set of rules. They help us know ourselves by something bigger than us, and the something bigger is relatively simple and not as complex as a real personality. So, because the Law is bigger than the individual, we can draw value and identity from it. But:

When you start drawing value and identity from Law, it has become your father and not your tutor.

And this is where Law, which was a good thing, becomes idolatry. Our identity should be found in *"God our Banner"* (Exodus 17:15). He is our identity because we carry His image. And He is our source of value because He has put His image on us. The bank notes in my wallet are worth nothing as pieces of paper, but the official use of the Queen's image links each note to the wealth of the whole nation. Jesus in us links us to the wealth of heaven.

So here we all stand in Christ. We all have a bit of legalism in us because we have all learnt the basics of "morality" without the Holy Spirit's help. But to really enter the Father's rest we need to let go of the things we do to earn His grace. If this were straightforward, more of us would have done it by now, but of course:

We don't get healed of legalism by trying to do the right thing.

The writer of Hebrews gives us an answer when he says:

"**Be quick to enter that rest**, *so no one should fall into their* [i.e. the wilderness Israelites] *pattern of unbelief.*" (Hebrews 4:11)

The word I have translated here as "quick" is often translated as "diligent." Both words together convey what I want to draw out of this answer. We need to get used to regularly "resting" in what God has done for us. We need to "be diligent" and we should do it as soon as possible! We need to "be quick". The longer we leave it and the less regular we are at it, the more chance there is that we will fall back into patterns of Law.

The writer of Hebrews expects that in this place of rest God will speak to us. So he continues in the next verse by explaining the effectiveness of the word of God and the ability of Jesus to cover our failings.

"*For the word of God is living, and active, and sharper than any two-edged sword, piercing even to the division of soul and spirit, of both joints and marrow, and is able to discern the thoughts and intentions of the heart.... So let's draw near to the throne of grace with boldness,* **so that we can get hold of mercy, and find grace to help as it is needed.**" (Hebrews 4:12,16)

There is nothing that should stop us entering God's rest, drawing near to His throne of grace. But we often don't do this when the rules we are living by tell us we are not good enough.

It is ironic that the very things that prevent us getting too intimate with God are the very things that His presence is likely to be fixing in us. The irony seems particularly heavy to me now, as I have discovered that the deepest intimacy with Jesus comes when I face the very worst of who I am with Him and find out that He just loves me even more deeply.

I used to either trivialise my sins or hide from Jesus when I was aware of them in me. Now I try to make myself totally transparent to Jesus, who sees through my coverings anyway! I try to let Him be my judge, my Saviour and my Redeemer all at the same time.

He can be all these things to me because He is the lover of my soul. **Love has two arms, the right one is called grace and the left is called truth and Jesus embraces you with both (John 1:17).**

Without the truth about you, you wouldn't understand the extravagance of His grace. There have been times when all I can do is cry with laughter at the ridiculously generous way that Jesus uses and honours me while, at the same time, His light reveals the hidden truth about me. Without grace I could never really face the difficult truth. There have also been times when I have wept in gratitude at His love for me, even when I am at my worst and most pompous and the consequences of sin's damage in me are painfully evident.

This is the intimacy of Sabbath rest. Like John, the disciple whom Jesus loved leaning back onto Jesus' breast as they ate the last supper while reclined at the table, this is what the sacrament of communion is prophesying to us every time we take it. Love reaches out in bread and wine with arms of grace and truth. The The bread speaks of fellowship but the wine reminds us what this cost.

That is why Paul says that some people have become sick and even died because they haven't honoured the communion meal (1 Corinthians 11:29-30). It is not that God has punished some people for not having clean hearts when they took communion. If you don't honour the prophetic sign you will not live in the intimate truth it is prophesying over you; and if you are not living in that intimacy you will slip back into Law; and if you live by the Law then, as Paul reminds us, you are under a curse and judgment (Galatians 3:10). A church that had in the past seen the sick healed (1 Corinthians 2:4-5) needed to understand why it had lost its favour with God.

I want to finish this chapter and the whole book with an example of the intimacy Jesus wants with us. But first, I want to consider two more issues related to Law. The first is an observation as to why so many Christians seem to get locked up under it, even when they don't want to. The second is to highlight how even the Law actually points us to a relationship beyond it.

Appealing to Caesar

"This man could have been set free if he had not appealed to Caesar." (Acts 26:32)

Agrippa spoke these words to Festus having heard Paul's defence of himself. Festus was in agreement, but Paul had appealed to Caesar and so to Caesar he had to go. I have this sneaky suspicion that many Christians get caught in Law because when it suits them they make an appeal to it, and once they have appealed to it they have put themselves under it's jurisdiction. When this happens it doesn't actually affect their relationship with Jesus and access to Him, but it does affect their ability to receive the grace God is giving them as favour. And if we don't see the evidence of favour on us it is not surprising if we start believing the world really is wired for justice over mercy, karma over grace. The devil's lies seem more real than heavenly truth.

So how do we appeal to the Law? Actually, almost anytime we make a judgment, even a kind one, on those around us we are appealing to Law. Which is why Jesus says, *"Don't judge, and you won't be judged, don't condemn and you won't be condemned, set free and you will be set free"* (Luke 6:37). It is possible to see truth without drawing judgment. It is possible to discern hearts without condemnation. You don't have to handcuff someone to the sin evident in them.

Passing judgment on someone is like reducing a person to a cartoon caricature. We have substituted the rich complex tapestry of desires, emotions experiences and dreams that make up a human being for a few crude defining lines. Once we have made a judgment we stop encountering the real person, we now see everything they do and everything they are through the thumbnail sketch we have created of them.

It is totally possible to discern and see truth without making a judgment. Discernment says, "That person is hurting", judgment says, "That's a hurt person". Discernment says, "That person doesn't always tell the truth", judgment says, "They are a liar".

Another way we appeal to Law is by holding on to our rights. There are no rights in faith other than the right to be a child of God (John 1:12). But Law establishes rights and requirements with every line. Rights are established by what the Law says I deserve and what I'm owed.

Unforgiveness is a right that is often held onto. Somebody once observed that: **"Unforgiveness is like drinking poison and hoping someone else dies."**

This is a very accurate description of what unforgiveness does to a person, which is why Jesus warns so strongly against it (Matthew 6:15).

But a word of caution is needed here. Because Christians have known for two millennia that they must forgive, the Church has come up with some very subtle counterfeit forms of forgiveness, reducing what is a miracle of grace to ways of controlling behaviour and pacifying emotions through subtle and seemingly kind judgments that help explain away real hurt.

Overt unforgiveness appeals to the rights implicit in Law, but fleshly forgiveness appeals to Law's judgment too, but in more subtle ways.

So we use judgments that balance a victim's failings against the failings in the persecutor that needs forgiving. If the difference is not too big the victim can muster up enough superiority to overlook the offence and mark down an emotional debit owed to them by the other party.

Or we use judgments that lock an offender's present behaviour patterns into the misfortunes of their past. In doing so we find a way of making their offenses acceptable to us as we balance our feeling of being sorry for them against the pain they cause us and others.

Both of these are simply *"holding a form of godliness while denying it's power"* (2 Timothy 3:5). By undermining real responsibility for sin in others we are subtly excusing ourselves from the need for forgiveness. The real power to forgive others comes from the power we receive in our own forgiveness.

Real forgiveness requires a work of grace in you to give it. Often you have to choose to forgive someone first as an act of will and faith, then the grace that empowers your choice follows later. To forgive is divine, but fortunately we are partakers in His divine nature.

I've used a couple of illustrations of the way in which we appeal to Law, but two millennia of infection of the Christian Church with the leaven of the Pharisees has produced a multitude of spiritual-looking legal appeals. It is the Spirit who leads you into truth and so I will commend you to His excellent guidance to help you see where you are putting yourself under the Law by your appeals to Caesar. Come out from under the legal umbrella and you will no doubt start to experience increased favour as the rain of grace starts soaking into your life again.

The Ten Commandments - A Charter for Relationship

"Tell me, you that desire to be under the law, don't you listen to the law?" (Galatians 4:21)

Jesus once pointed out that all Scripture pointed the reader towards Him (John 5:39). Discovering Jesus on every line of the Old Testament has been a passion of mine since I first noticed Jesus' claim back in 1989. But here all I want to do is highlight how the Law all points towards relationship.

What we call the "Ten Commandments" are actually never called that in the Bible. They are always referred to as the "ten words" in both the Hebrew Old Testament and it's Greek translation the Septuagint. The closest the Old Testament comes to calling them commandments is in Deuteronomy where it says literally,

"He declared His covenant to you, which He commanded you to accomplish. Ten words He wrote on two tablets of stone." (Deuteronomy 4:13)

So even here (when you read what the Hebrew text says without adding unnecessary words), the idea of "commandment" is only loosely associated with the "ten words" or what theologians call the Decalogue and that most of us learnt as the Ten Commandments.

By the time of the New Testament every line of the books of Moses had been sifted for "commandments" and these ten words of God's grace were now viewed as commands - although the New Testament still uses a softer word that can mean a "charge" or a "precept" when it refers to these specific instructions in the Law.

These words were given after 19 chapters worth of God's grace and it is interesting how, if we approach them as *"words of grace that have the power to build you up"* (Act 20:34), they read much more like promises than commandments.

The last of the ten words is actually quite hard to interpret as a commandment because it is a statement about our hearts' emotions: *"You shall not covet...".* As a command this is hard to keep if you have an envious heart, but as a promise it is very liberating: "You will be free from envy."

When you look at the rest of the "ten words" you can't help noticing that almost all of the actual words that make them up are spent on how to relate to God. 74% of the words in fact.

This all makes sense in the light of the New Testament. It is what Paul knows, it is what Jesus taught. If you get your relationship with heaven sorted out everything else will fall into line. Outside of the relationship with heaven, what should be promises will just become burdens.

God commanded His people to keep the covenant, i.e. to stay faithful in relationship with Him. Within this "marriage" He had issued ten words that, if the relationship worked, would happen. Biblical archaeology has now discovered the basic form of the marriage vow used by Semitic peoples in biblical times. These also contained words that were both promises and commands at the same time. These promise words included the provision of food, clothing and love, but it was understood that these would emerge from the relationship by cooperation. So the husband would provide meat and grain by his labour and the wife would prepare edible cooked meals. The relationship had provided food. The husband would provide animal skins and raw fibres, the wife would spin, cut, weave and sew and produce garments. The relationship had provided clothing. And as to love, well as they say, it takes two to tango.

Marriage was the most common form of a Covenant agreement in the ancient world. It should have demonstrated to the children of Israel that the words God spoke into His covenant with them were only possible out of relational faithfulness, just as was true in marriage. But where a relationship has broken down, all that is left is a legal framework. When there is no real relationship we still have rules. And this was the state Judaism was in when Jesus came into the world to create a New Covenant between heaven and earth.

This new Covenant was different to the first in that, whereas the first Covenant was based on mutual faithfulness, this one would be based on God's faithfulness alone. God would create a way to wipe out the consequences of mans unfaithfulness (Jeremiah 31:31-35), so that every single person could really "know the Lord". In this new Covenant, God's words would get into the hearts of people (Jeremiah 31:33).

Relationship was fundamental to the success of the Old Covenant, but without the means of fully dealing with sin once and for all, the relationship was limited in its intimacy. The romantic meal was continually punctuated by the need to wash dishes.

Relationship is fundamental to the New Covenant too, but the work of the cross has removed every barrier and separation between each and every person and our loving God. Sin is no longer a separation and if we will be "diligent" and "quick" to use the access we have to rest in Him, then we will find His promises get written onto our hearts and there is no need for Law.

Dinner for Two

"You prepare a table before me in the presence of my enemies. You anoint my head with oil. My cup runs over." (Psalm 23:5)

Over a year I try to create a schedule of life that will include dedicated retreats with Jesus. Sometimes these retreats can seem indulgent, but that misses the high value Jesus puts on times of intimacy with us. As I have seen a prophetic ministry grow in me I have been so pleasantly challenged to see what incredible lengths Jesus will go to, simply to set up an encounter moment with someone that makes perfect sense to them, even if it makes very little difference to the world outside.

In addition, every couple of years I try to take and extended prayer retreat, often combining it with a trip to somewhere I would like to visit or where I might connect with someone from whom I want to receive.

A few years ago I went to Bethel Church in Redding, California, both to take time with Jesus at their prayer centre, but also to meet the leader there, Bill Johnson.

I arrived in San Francisco in the early evening and drove three hours north to Ukiah and crashed out in cheap motel. I was so tired that even though the walls were paper thin and there were noisy families on both sides of me, I slept soundly. The next day I cut across country to join the northern Californian coast road. I knew the coastline would be stunning and I would see the delight of Jesus in creation as I headed for the town of Eureka, 300 miles to the north.

I spent an incredible day with Jesus, not praying about specific agendas just really enjoying His presence and being moved to tears by the beauty of creation all around me. There were times when His presence in the car was tangible.

One particular moment stands out. My journey took me through the giant redwoods of Humboldt Park. As I drove off the main freeway to join the winding scenic road called, "The Avenue of the Giants", I was hit by the presence of Jesus. It was so real and intense that it made me cry out loud as I drove and I had to pull in to the side of the road. I realised that I had been hit by this wave of love that was causing my body to tingle and twitch just as I had driven past the sign that read, "Welcome to Humboldt Park" and so I asked Jesus "why"? And immediately the phrase "Jesus is sneaking through Humboldt Park" came into my head and I was hit by laughter and joy, though I will need to explain why.

A month or so before my trip to the US I had had an encounter with Jesus while on a course run by my friends Stephen and Mara. The course was to help people to encounter Jesus with a view to understanding themselves better. I was in partnership with Judith my wife who had been asking me questions about what I was seeing and hearing as I let the Spirit speak to me. I had seen myself walking with Jesus and being shown lots of doors. Jesus was encouraging me to open them. So Judith asked me, "What happens when you open one?" In the picture I was having I stepped forward and opened a door. As the door opened Jesus, (who had been standing just behind me, encouraging me to open a door) suddenly jumped through the door making jazz hands and shouted "Surprise!" I was so shocked I physically reacted and then started to laugh uncontrollably. Judith was trying to ask me what was happening and I was struggling to say, "Jesus ... He ... said ...

'surprise!'" As Judith pieced together what happened she started laughing too. It may seem irreligious, but this was the picture I had. I knew that the Lord was saying that I get real joy from exploring with Him and then being surprised by Him and of course it's the "joy of the Lord" that is our strength.

Fast forward to a couple of months later. I've travelled half way round the world, driven for half a day and, as I cross the line into Humboldt Park, Jesus really had jumped out from behind the welcome sign and said "surprise!"

But more than that, I knew where the phrase "Jesus is sneaking through Humboldt Park" came from! When I was ten years old I had found a book called *Faith, Hope and Hilarity*, supposedly written by Dick Van Dyke (better known for his bad cockney accent in such classic films as *Mary Poppins* and *Bedknobs and Broomsticks* than his spiritual insights). The book was full of supposedly true and funny stories of US church life. The only story I can actually remember from this profound tome was of a boy who had thought that the hymn, "Jesus is seeking a humble heart" started with the words, "Jesus is sneaking through Humboldt Park". As a ten-year old I had laughed, even though I had no idea where or what a Humboldt Park was.

Now here I was at forty years old enjoying a moment of pure indulgent joy as Jesus brought together my hopes for my time away, an encounter experience from a month or so beforehand and half remembered pleasures from a distant childhood. In that moment just behind the welcome sign at the southern end of the "Avenue of the Giants", I knew the truth of communion with Jesus. A communion not based on doing, but on simply being with Him.

I could tell you so many others stories, not just mine but stories that others I know have experienced which demonstrate how much time and effort Jesus puts into those moments that affirm your value to Him. Most of these stories could be treated as trivial, but they are not to the people who experience them. God doesn't give them as proofs for those that don't want to believe. They are examples of the compassion and goodness of God that interrupts people's lives with gifts of love, affection, encouragement and confirmation.

Creation is desperate for messengers who can mediate tangible tokens of Father's love to a hurting world. "God is Love" is the most profound and fundamental statement that can be made about God's existential nature. "Jesus loves you" is the most freeing truth in the universe. But love that is only ever expressed in generalities is a contradiction in terms. Love has to get personal and intimate. *"We love..."* writes John (the disciple whom Jesus loved), *"...because He loved us first!"* (1 John 4:19).

In Mark and Matthew we read about how the Pharisees come and ask Jesus for a "sign" (Matthew 16:1, Mark 8:11). In the preceding chapters Jesus has fed 5,000 plus people, walked on water, walked through crowds of sick people healing them as they touched His cloak, the dumb have spoken the blind have seen, the demonically oppressed have been freed and then He's just fed another 4,000 or more. All through these narratives the Pharisees have been popping up with "concerns": His disciples picked some grain on the Sabbath, they didn't wash their hands properly etc.

Now when they ask Jesus for a sign, Jesus replies that *"no sign will be given this generation"* (Mark 8:12). In Matthew He adds, *"except the sign of Jonah"* (Matthew 16:4) referring cryptically to His resurrection. The resurrection was to be a sign to all people in all places, but Jesus doesn't bother to refer the Pharisees to all the healings and miracles of all the previous chapters because they where not done as generic signs, they were given as individual love gifts to their individual recipients. Of course, they would also be precious moments to those who loved and knew the recipient of each heavenly gift. To the Pharisees they meant nothing and Jesus wasn't going to do miracles to convince the sceptics. But He would be moved by compassion to demonstrate the love of God to those who needed to know it. If you think about it, one of the most famous prophecies in Scripture was actually given not for the unbelieving world, nor really for God's people generally, it was given for a frightened, sixteen-year-old girl.

"Look, I see the virgin shall conceive and have a son and they will call his name 'God with us.'" (Isaiah 7:14)

Look at the verses just before this and you'll see that this prophecy was given as a sign (v11) into a specific context (v13): *"hear oh house of David."* To a world that doesn't believe, the story of Jesus' conception and virgin birth is a nice religious fable; it convinces nobody, they all know where babies come from. But it wasn't primarily given for the world, it was given for the house of David, for His physical descendants.

Both Mary and Joseph were descendants of David. Matthew gives Joseph's genealogy and Luke gives Mary's. Mary is the only person in all of history who, in the flesh, can really know the truth of her virginity at the time of Jesus' conception. So can you imagine how important a sign Isaiah's prophecy would have been to her as she faced shame, gossip and speculation at best, or a life shunned and alone or even stoning? Mary must have drawn on these words and the surrounding passages of Isaiah as she watched the events of Jesus' life unfold.

The word would also have spoken to Joseph, although he could only receive its truth by faith. God graciously confirmed the matter to him by three witnesses: Mary's testimony, the angelic dream and Isaiah's prophetic word, specifically given for Joseph as a descendant of David.

Then there are those of us who are prophetically of the house of the Messiah (i.e. followers of Jesus). We can see the virgin birth as a rationally consistent sign of who Jesus is. After all, if He is both Son of God and Son of Man, how else would we expect Him to enter the world. The prophecy fits our expectations, but it doesn't impact us like it must have impacted Mary.

But for those who do not want to believe, the virgin birth is not a sign at all, Jesus was just another baby with dubious parentage.

You see these verses that bless us as they are read out each Christmas were primarily given for a young Palestinian girl, frightened about what the Lord was doing in her. They are an expression of the kindness of God to an individual.

The more I read Scripture, the more I see that the individual is often the primary focus of God's attention - hence all those lists of names. The fact that by faith these people's stories speak to us too is almost incidental. If history is defined by wars, conquests, explorations and inventions, then "His story" is defined by billions of unique lives each carrying a testimony of a love forged in adversity. You are the "apple of His eye", the filter He sees the world through.

As the apple of His eye, the Father is more concerned with the person you are becoming than He is about the things you want to do for Him. He will prepare things for you to do if you will walk with Him into the broad horizon of Christ.

To End

"May the God of peace Himself completely sanctify you. May your whole spirit, soul, and body be kept blameless in the presencing of our Lord Jesus Christ."[2] (1 Thessalonians 5:23)

The supra-natural life is not something to do. It is something that flows out of those who are being shaped by God in their souls as well as in their spirits. This is God's work, but we can cooperate with Him to release more of it now.

In this book I have only tried to cover what I consider to be the key practices and dynamics of being shaped and grown by the Holy Spirit. In many ways we have only considered the principles that get us to the Jordan ready to enter our promises. We have not yet looked at how to live once we are in the Promised Land. That is a subject for others books in this series. But the principles addressed in this book don't stop once you have crossed the Jordan.

My prayer is that the lessons and teaching contained in this book will act a travel guide to make you want to explore further the undiscovered country of your life in Christ Jesus.

Why not take time now to ask Him about your future?

Endnotes:

1. The Banner or Standard that an army marched under was a symbol of its identity.

2. Usual translations of this verse will read "at the coming of our Lord Jesus Christ". The translation I have used is legitimate and reflects my conviction that the early Church used the word *"parousia"* for the second coming of Jesus because it connected the future event to their present reality. *"Parousia"* means more literally "presence" or "presencing" and the early Church knew the experience of Jesus' presence in their midst.

About the Author

Christen Forster is the Senior Leader of River, an emerging connection of churches and ministries coming out of River Church in the Thames Valley. Christen passed on the practical leadership of River Church in 2010 to take on this wider role, which also allows him to minister more widely. He combines powerful personal testimony and fresh, applicable teaching with an emphasis on the prophetic and healing.

Christen is a second generation church leader, the son of Roger and Faith Forster, and has planted churches, led youth and evangelism programmes, missions teams and congregations. As a 15-year old he was diagnosed with terminal non-Hodgkin's Lymphoma, but was supernaturally healed. In the late 1980s Christen spent time at the Fuller Seminary in Pasadena under Peter Wagner, being taught by John Wimber and Rick Warren among others. Here he met and lived with Ché Ahn, founder of Harvest International Ministries.

In the 1990s Christen started and ran the Challenge 2000 project, a UK expression of the international DAWN Strategy for saturation church planting. DAWN was linked with the "AD 2000 and Beyond Movement" and in this role he led the UK delegation to the Global Congress on World Evangelism in Seoul, Korea and organised several large prayer and leadership events in the UK. During this period Christen co-authored a book, *Small Church, Big Vision* with International Director of YWAM, Lynn Green. In the late 1990s Christen and his family moved to Maidenhead where he eventually took on the leadership of River Church. It was here that the Lord turned Christen's understanding of the Christian life upside down and the church came into a broad experience of widespread healing and prophetic transformation.